Praise for *Under A Blue Moon*

"After years of admiring Isa for her myriad physical achievements as world class skier and climber, my respect now deepens as I watch her seek and experience truths that seem to stem from the non-physical realms.

She now gives this book as a gift to us all; a peek into the experiences of one who says 'Yes' to life. May it guide many to changed perspectives and uplifted spirits, as her whole being has done for me."

- Colette Foster, Professor of Mathematics

"When given the privilege to read an advance copy of the book, I didn't know what to expect. From the very first page, the reader becomes immersed in a year long journey that is part adventure, part educational, part magical and ultimately mystical. Some of the stories shared in the book may seem hard to believe, but having known Isa for years, I have no doubt that the experiences recounted did indeed take place. Beware. If one reads "Under A Blue Moon," your perception of the world will be altered forever. And not a moment too soon."

- Kevin Griffin, VT Superior Court Judge

"I have been thinking that the narratives in both Wild and Eat, Pray, Love begin when the authors had reached a very low point in their lives; the low point was their crisis, and the journey their path to the transformation they desperately needed. Isa Oehry's life was different; she recognized all its good qualities, while believing a change was needed – but what? Her crisis point was in realizing that the very security and safety of her life may have been holding her back in a

spiritual search – and the realization came with the point of an arrow against her neck!

In spite of hesitations or fears she may have had at that moment, she, like Elizabeth Gilbert and Cheryl Strayed, knew that only by taking risks could she move forward."

- Dorothy Gannon, Editor

"With her book, "Under A Blue Moon," Isa has provided me with a valuable resource in my quest to better understand my life on this earth. As a mountain guide, it's critical for me to make the right decision at the right time. Under pressure in life and death situations, remaining relaxed helps to make the right choice. By using the techniques Isa describes in her book, I am better able to remain relaxed and fully aware of my surroundings, helping me to be a better and safer guide."

- Hans Solmssen - Mountain Guide

Under a Blue Moon

Isabella S. Oehry

BALBOA.
PRESS

A DIVISION OF HAY HOUSE

Balboa Press books may be ordered through booksellers or by contacting:

Balboa Press
A Division of Hay House
1663 Liberty Drive
Bloomington, IN 47403
www.balboapress.com
1 (877) 407-4847

Because of the dynamic nature of the Internet, any web addresses or
links contained in this book may have changed since publication and
may no longer be valid. The views expressed in this work are solely those
of the author and do not necessarily reflect the views of the publisher,
and the publisher hereby disclaims any responsibility for them.

The author of this book does not dispense medical advice or prescribe the use
of any technique as a form of treatment for physical, emotional, or medical
problems without the advice of a physician, either directly or indirectly. The
intent of the author is only to offer information of a general nature to help
you in your quest for emotional and spiritual well-being. In the event you use
any of the information in this book for yourself, which is your constitutional
right, the author and the publisher assume no responsibility for your actions.

Any people depicted in stock imagery provided by Thinkstock are
models, and such images are being used for illustrative purposes only.
Certain stock imagery © Thinkstock.

Print information available on the last page.

ISBN: 978-1-5043-3910-0 (sc)
ISBN: 978-1-5043-3912-4 (hc)
ISBN: 978-1-5043-3911-7 (e)

Library of Congress Control Number: 2015914298

Balboa Press rev. date: 12/07/2015

2nd edition, December 2015

CONTENTS

PART III

PART IV

PART V

This book is dedicated to my mother, a woman with unquenchable determination and a heart of gold, a woman who showed me how to walk fearlessly through life by her example.

And to my father, a wise fighter for human rights and a gentle soul who introduced me to the beauty and mystery of nature, a man who brought to my mind first moments of true and silencing awe.

The most beautiful experience
we can have
is the mysterious.
It is the fundamental emotion
that stands at the cradle
of true art
and true science.

—Albert Einstein (1879–1955)

Let us leave nothing untried for
nothing happens by itself:
All men's gains
are the fruit of adventure.

—Herodotus (484–425 BC)
Greek historian

FOREWORD

The first time I met Isa, I was very impressed with the positive energy that surrounded her presence. I knew in my first brief visit with her that I had met a very special person. I was to find out that Isa is Liechtenstein born and raised. Liechtenstein is a country whose total population is somewhere around thirty-seven thousand people. What are the chances of meeting someone from Liechtenstein who is now living in the hills of Vermont? And the intrigue really started to swirl when I found out that Isa is a multiple world championship medalist! It is no wonder that she brings vitality to the room and now to her book.

Under a Blue Moon is a refreshing look at Isa's thoughts and activities. She plays with scientific ideas that seem to bring mystery to her everyday life. This book is a real joy to read. You may well find yourself researching any or all of the many queries Isa brings to her adventures. The activities alone lead us on interesting and exciting journeys, such as mountain and ice climbing. Add to this Isa's curious and scientific mind, and an almost childlike and insatiable inquisitiveness, and you want to hear more with each passing chapter. Enjoy this romp with Isa. It leaves you yearning for more of her playful outlook on life.

I hope you someday have the pleasure of meeting my new friend. Then you, too, can experience the energy that travels with her mentally and physically. *Under a Blue Moon* delivers to you a bit of her insights while you are engrossed in the merrymaking flow of life. *Enjoy!*

—Mark A. Wisniewski, DDS, AIAOMT, AAO
Greenfield, MA

PREFACE

In the pages to follow, you will learn about a true and extraordinary journey that began innocently under the golden light of a full moon. Mysteriously nourished, enriched, and highly energized by an unknown force while I was floating on water under the brilliant light of a blue moon, I felt a prompting inviting me to a destination yet unknown, a hidden world concealing ancient wisdom. I spontaneously decided to set out to find it.

My search led me into a world where people, according to the laws of science, have no right to be alive. My eyes were opened to previously unknown ideas and what at first sight appear as unbelievable truths. Understanding, as I had been taught about this earth, its people, animals, and plants—the entire universe—suddenly no longer applied.

I followed the call to mountaintops and ascended frozen cliffs thousands of feet tall. At times, I was engulfed in mysterious worlds of minerals and plants. Then again, I found myself in the arms of passion so all-encompassing, it overrode all sense of logic and reason. Yet, as if guided by an unseen hand, secrets revealed themselves while I remained unharmed. Longing to learn and understand even more, I ventured into the mountains high above and beyond where mankind lives and journeyed to the hidden gates of the legendary worlds. Under a canopy of millions of blinking stars, I asked permission to enter, and then it happened.

I knew that the insights I gained were not meant for me alone. I hope my personal journey will inspire you as well. It may forever change how you view the world you live in.

ACKNOWLEDGMENTS

By documenting what took place, I hoped that others might be inspired to look beyond the obvious and keep their minds and hearts open for the unseen and the previously unheard. For those skeptical readers—whom I applaud, for it is my conviction that you should not believe anything unless you have experienced it yourself—I encourage to bear with me when things seem to get a little wild and crazy. Yet I have experienced everything the way I recorded it in the pages to follow. Besides looking at life through a humorous lens at times, nothing has been embellished or added.

What I did not know at the beginning of this endeavor was that it takes an entire town full of people to not only raise a child but also to write a book. So many have supported this process knowingly—and often unknowingly—simply by being part of my journey.

Special thanks go out to my friend Colette Foster. I will never forget our heartfelt laughter while I was working through the first and quite raw version of the manuscript. Your emotional support was invaluable and your insights and patience were a precious gift. Later I put the loose pages into the hands of my fabulous editor, Dorothy Gannon. In her gentle and tactful ways, she helped me to refine my grasp of the intricacies of English, my second language, without ever taking away my own voice, or becoming impatient with this enthusiastic yet challenging debut author. I especially thank my friends and companions on this journey–Alexander, Tim, and Ernie. It was through our adventures we experienced together that I was able to learn and grow. I will be forever grateful for your presence in my life. Your names have been changed to assure privacy. I am also grateful to the many friends who continued to ask me about the progress of my book, especially friends like Peter, who purchased a copy more than a year prior to the book's publication. Your interest in and curiosity about what I could possibly be writing was an inspiration and motivation.

In my research I have discovered many distinguished writers and scientists whose work I deeply respect and often reference in my writing. However, should you find a speck of wisdom in this book in addition to their contribution, do not believe that it stems from me at all. I merely narrated my adventures as I experienced them during this extraordinary year. For deeper insights and wisdom, I gratefully handed over my pen to those who have already come and gone. These are the special men and women who have walked this earth before us and experienced the same struggles before they finally won their freedom from rebirth. They are known as teachers and masters. As I marked each day of this journey, beginning at day one and scribbling all the way through day 365 on my little piece of scrap paper, I became more and more aware of the presence of these incredibly wise beings and their deep love for all of us here on earth. They generously want to share their wisdom with those who are willing and eager to listen and learn. My gratitude to them and my trust in their guidance deepened each day.

In my writing I have used the term *man* when I refer to the human species, male or female, and I have substituted "he or she" with *he* to make writing and reading easier. At all times in such cases, please remember that I am addressing both sexes. In the back I have added a list of suggested scholastic research topics that I touch upon in the text. There is no need for me to go into detail about these topics, as each can easily be verified and researched at a deeper level. Each topic alone would warrant an entire book by itself.

And finally whenever one "hangs his soul like a piece of laundry into the wind" as I am doing with this book, one is naturally subjected to the wind's abuse. I understand that this book is not for everyone. I hope, however, if you are one of the readers who cannot relate to my experiences, you will be gentle with me. At the very least, you might enjoy hearing about my adventures and experience a taste of living through the various seasons in Vermont.

PART I

INTRODUCTION

An Auspicious Night: The Beginning of a Remarkable Journey

Avoiding unnecessary noise, I slipped into my canoe, placed myself in the middle, and braced my bare knees firmly against its sides. I pushed off. It was dark, so far a moonless sky. Instantly I felt at one with my vessel, enjoying the sensation of my canoe's response to the slightest and most subtle movements of my body. I glided with ease. I loved that feeling.

It was an auspicious night. After I had finished my work for the day, I had driven to my favorite body of water, the Green River Reservoir in northern Vermont. As always, I had brought my canoe and had packed food and water. I had arrived just before dark, the mysterious time at water's edge when daylight changes and bright colors turn to multiple variations of soft pales. A time, when the fading evening colors and the last pink in the sky transform into infinite shades of gray and then black. By now it was so dark, I could barely recognize the difference between the water and the shore.

It was an exceptionally warm night. I wore only a couple of pieces of fabric that surely would not have qualified as clothing in most countries of this world. I wanted to be as close to the elements as possible. The water was smooth, an ocean of absolute blackness. It revealed no sign of depth. It seemed a gaping and bottomless abyss with an unknown world of life and creatures below, a world from which only my canoe separated me. I glided toward the openness of the reservoir, leaving the shore far behind. In anticipation of what I had set out to witness, I had no thoughts of fear.

Then the first signs of the rising moon began to color the eastern sky. From the middle of the large body of water, I had an unobstructed view of this breathtaking spectacle.

First the sky turned lighter in color where the moon was about to appear. Then the area on the horizon intensified, announcing its imminent arrival. And finally the first flecks began to emerge, forming a brilliant orb in the sky. The moon rose more quickly than I had expected. It was huge, a magnificent lantern reflecting itself in the black water before me. A golden path—its reflection—tied it to the tip of my canoe. Whichever way I aimed my vessel, the path, like a golden fabric, was always a straight line between the moon and myself. Like Dorothy in Oz, I followed the yellow brick road.

Occasionally a soft breeze stirred the mirrorlike water and sent ripples over the brilliant reflection. The warm air gently caressed my bare skin. I felt a pleasant tension building like a soft electrical current while all the little hairs on my body reached out like antennas, eager to receive some unknown signals. It keenly sharpened my senses. I let the moonlight soak into the very core of my bones. I absorbed it through my skin and breathed it with each breath. It was a surreal experience. I was not alone, however. The hooting of the great horned owl, the calling of the loon, and the thunderous clap of the beaver's tail accompanied me. The animals did not seem to be concerned with sleep either. We all were in awe of this fabulous lunar display. I paddled for hours, transfixed by the experience.

This was not only a full moon but also a blue moon, not to mention my birthday moon. A blue moon is a rare event. It is commonly known as a second full moon within the same month. The Metonic cycle, as lunar phases are termed, is a nineteen-year-long cycle. Within nineteen years there are 228 calendar months, and because calendar months are longer than moon cycles, which are on average only 29.53 days long, it so happens that at least eight times within a Metonic cycle, we experience two full moons in one month. The second full moon is called a blue moon.

But even more exceptional is a blue moon on your birthday. Blue moons can only happen on the thirtieth or thirty-first of a month. It was August 31, my birthday, and with a full moon, a blue moon, and a birthday moon, a special celebration was in order. I wanted to connect with my three moons in a way that would be memorable. I had absolutely no idea at the time how unforgettable this night would become. All I knew was that I was soaking in more than what my eyes could see, my skin could feel, and my mind could possibly conjure up on its own. My soul was dining lusciously on some mystical food. I was being nourished and enriched cosmically. I had no desires or longings. I found myself deeply peaceful, incredibly happy, and fully satisfied.

The next morning by the water's edge, feeling highly energized and alert, I knew I wanted more of this food. I wanted to know where it came from and if it was possible to tap into it at will. I suspected that whatever it was I had been absorbing by lunar spoonfuls the previous night, it could nourish me completely, satisfy me mentally and emotionally, and possibly even accomplish much more. With absolute certainty and determination, I decided on the spot to dedicate a year to the research and discovery of this mystical nourishment. Without any idea at the time of how this journey was going to unfold, what adventures would take place, and to what unexpected insights and discoveries it would lead me, I knew it would be worth the effort.

Prana: Light Energy

I had heard of this food before and had tasted it in bits much like a little cosmic treat. It is known as prana, light energy. *Prana* is the Sanskrit name for life force or cosmic energy. This all-pervading cosmic energy has already been described in the *Vedas*, sacred texts among the oldest on earth. Legend states that prana is responsible for life itself, is ever-existent and ever-abundantly available. It is said that it can lead to infinite wisdom. One could exist on prana *alone.*

I wanted to know if the legend was true. I was curious to find out whether prana could really nourish me beyond my exceptional full-moon night. During the night, while floating on water, I had enjoyed more than a taste, and I was deeply intrigued. I wanted to find out for myself, and I made up my mind. I was going to do whatever was necessary to seduce prana into my being.

Not eating food was not the goal. Instead I wished for prana to satisfy my inner hungers. These were not necessarily the growling of the stomach but my soul's hunger for a deeper understanding of life. It was the hunger of my cells to express themselves in perfection and eliminate disease by doing so. It was the hunger of my mind for clarity and the hunger for emotional satisfaction and inner peace. I wanted to know if it was possible to achieve freedom from any lack, fear, or maybe even aging and dying. I wanted to know a human being's full potential. I wanted to know the truth about life, all of it. As a very wise person once proclaimed, "The truth will set you free."

I figured that if I knew the deepest truths about life, not only would it help me along my personal journey, but I would also be able to help others. I remembered waking up early one morning and lying in bed, contemplating the beautiful day that was about to unfold. A sunny and warm day was predicted. I could not go to work that day because a deliveryman was coming to my house and I had to be present. I knew I would begin the day with a meditation and follow it with a breakfast outside on my deck. I imagined how the sun would warm my face while I ate among beautiful flowers and chirping birds. During the day I would have time to read and write, work in the garden, go for a run if I chose, and jump in the pond to cool off. And there was going to be time to play my fiddle. I did not have to leave my house or use my car, which was another bonus for a glorious day. I was healthy. I had enough food, and my few bills were paid. I had no personal worries. However, as I envisioned this day, I realized that although deeply grateful for it, I was for some strange reason not overflowing with happiness and joy. *Why not?* I asked myself. Why would I not want to scream out loud with joy and delight? Why was I not completely in a state of bliss? I lay in bed, contemplating. I scrutinized my thoughts and my feelings and came again to the conclusion that as long as there was suffering in the hearts of my loved ones, a cloud would always cover my own happiness. My happiness was ultimately connected to those around me. Their pain reached my heart as well. Convinced that we were all connected in some mysterious way, I knew that reaching my own personal state of bliss and peace was only the beginning. Not until suffering had ceased was ultimate bliss and lasting peace a possibility.

Even as a toddler, I remember—like many others before me have done—being deeply connected with something much greater than myself. I felt as though I was a small piece that had inadvertently tumbled out of a very large puzzle. This piece, unique in its shape and shades of color, did not fit into the framework of my earthly family very well. But I knew instinctively that it fit perfectly into a much larger picture apart from this visible world. In this picture I was truly home and deeply and unconditionally loved. No suffering existed. Throughout my life I always felt this connection and delved deeper into the search for its origin with each passing year. As a teenager, I often went climbing in the Alps by myself in search for it. I would reach the top of a mountain that was marked with a huge cross twenty feet tall in the European tradition, sit next to it, and ponder. Here I would experience my first moments of meditation. High up in the mountains far above the often still sleepy towns, I would feel a little closer to this *something*.

As an adult, I studied clinical psychology to better understand the human mind. I engrossed myself in the study of comparative religion and death and dying in search of a better understanding of the human soul. Eventually I recognized myself as a seeker, someone who would not rest until she understood her spiritual origin. I wanted to know the truth about life. Then and only then, I would finally be able to understand others, the origin of suffering, the state of lasting bliss, and ultimately, myself.

Prana promised to answer my questions. I decided that the first step was to find out if others had succeeded in receiving, absorbing and enjoying the many wonderful benefits of prana. I found that history is scattered with legendary people, who seemed to have succeeded in absorbing some sort of life-sustaining energy. Astonishingly, they had no need for physical nourishment and often were granted outstanding wisdom and abilities. According to the laws of science, these people had no right to be alive. Their cases of course were highly controversial. And in the absence of a scientific explanation, we resolved the mystery by simply declaring them to be saints.

Not feeling too saintly myself and thoroughly enjoying nature's bounty, I pondered if there was a way that I could possibly benefit from these people's experiences and wisdom.

Morphic Fields

In 2012, the One Laptop per Child organization (OLPC), an organization that aims at providing the world's poorest children with laptops designed for self-empowered learning, went to two remote villages in Ethiopia. The youngsters at these villages had no previous exposure to written words of their own language or to the alphabet, let alone the English language, computers, or cell phones. OLPC dropped off taped boxes containing preloaded tablet computers. The tablets, which were programmed in English, contained alphabet-training games, e-books, movies, cartoons, paintings, a camera function that was disabled, and many other programs, but there were no instructions.

Within four minutes of dropping off the boxes, one child had opened a box, found the on-off switch, and powered up the first tablet. Five days later the children were using forty-seven apps per child per day. Two weeks later they were singing the ABC songs in the village. The camera in the computers had been disabled, but within five months the children figured it out and hacked Android. OLPC reported that they had made efforts to freeze the desktop settings. But the children had managed to hack around the frozen settings and completely customized the desktops so each child's tablet had a different look.

We know that children learn with ease compared to adults. However, had we given our great-grandparents' generation these tablets when they were children, would they have progressed as fast as these children did? Rupert Sheldrake, a cell biologist proposes that a force exists that connects each individual with all other individuals in its species. He goes even further and suggests that each species has a "group mind" upon which each individual draws upon but also contributes. He terms this force "morphic field." Behavior, thoughts, and habits of any given species build up in these fields over time and generations. They then affect the members of the same species living today. Sheldrake suggests that in this way, new patterns of behavior can spread faster and easier.

A Harvard psychologist named William McDougall accidentally tested this theory over a period of thirty-four years. He trained rats to complete a maze with electrified hazards and quickly discovered that later generations of rats completed the maze more quickly than preceding generations. The twenty-second generation of rats in the study figured the maze out ten times as fast as the first generation. But more astounding was that McDougall discovered that rats from untrained genetic lines that had no contact with the trained rats displayed the same rate of improvement. The improvement manifested itself in the rat species *en masse*, which contradicted the theory that the information was passed down genetically. This was truly a remarkable discovery. How did the rats become "smarter" on their own over time without training?

Sheldrake believes that each species has its own morphic field and that species members can tune into or share in this field. These fields are constantly changing and absorbing new information, and they are not subject to the laws of time and space. In the case of the rats, rat species not included in McDougall's experiment could, according to Sheldrake, tap into the morphic field of rats and learn from their relatives without having physical contact with them. At the time of death, a being's habits, thoughts, and behavior are not lost but merge with that being's morphic field, states Sheldrake, and these are accessible to future generations of the same species.

By tapping into morphic subfields, which are more specific fields that include even nonliving things, knowledge could be gained about any subject, suggests Sheldrake. Absorbing prana must then have its own morphic subfield. By immersing myself into the research of prana, I could tap into its morphic field and benefit from all who have traveled this path before me. Like the rats in the laboratory, the children in Ethiopia, even the legendary saints, I could learn much more quickly using information of morphic fields as "the wind under my wings."

Part II

Fall

Messages From The Other Side

A couple weeks had already passed since my commitment to this journey. It was September, Vermont's most glorious season. Vermont is called the Green Mountain State, and most of our green is due to forests covering the rolling hills. In early September, the leaves of deciduous trees begin to turn color, changing from deep green to every variation of yellow, gold, orange, and red. This display of nature begins in the north with the first cold nights and slowly moves south over the entire state, lasting well into October. Finally everything is aglow. It takes your breath away year after year. Folks from all over the world travel here to get a look. Locals call these visitors "leaf-peepers." Since my moonlight adventure in late August, fall had advanced, and nights had become colder. Forests had transformed into a brilliant and breathtaking spectacle.

One of the ultimate highlights of fall in Vermont is the famous World's Fair in the small town of Tunbridge. Anyone who has ever been to this fair wants to return. The name alone indicates that something extraordinary is happening here, or at least the townspeople may want you to think so. Every year for more than 140 years, the town of Tunbridge, claiming a population of roughly 1,500 people, hosts this event, attracting tens of thousands of visitors. The fair was once a wild place with topless girls dancing on hay wagons, while eager and often intoxicated farm boys fought over them. Today, although much calmer without any girlie shows, it still has a unique flair.

I had looked forward to the fair as I had every year since my first visit. Finally the day had arrived. By the time I crossed the narrow footbridge leading to the animal barns, it was already dark. I went straight to the oxen shelter. I loved the gentleness of these animals, and I never ceased to marvel at their enormous size. Tucked into their sleeping quarters, their huge bodies, too large to fit into the stall, reached far into the walkway. While I carefully passed behind, I tentatively touched them, and I was surprised anew at how warm and soft they felt and how relaxed they were. This seemed in direct contrast to the enormous strength and power they displayed while they were dragging huge blocks of cement during the ox pull.

Leaving the oxen to their well-deserved sleep, I wandered over to the cattle barns. Above the resting animals, many multicolored ribbons had proudly been attached to the rafters, displaying the day's accomplishments. Rosy-cheeked farm kids had themselves tucked in near their spotlessly cleaned cows. I slowed my gait when I passed these slumbering children. This was an idyllic sight that I treasured, reminiscent of another time long gone. Here in Vermont it still exists.

I continued my stroll to the poultry barns, which were well lit. Despite the late hour, sleep had not yet settled in amongst these feathery creatures. Roosters of all sizes and colors crowed in every octave, and geese, ducks, pigeons, and baby chicks joined the cacophony. It was truly a lively place with lots of bird talk going on. The bird conversations brought back a memory of an encounter I once had with such a feathery friend.

It was on a late September day, one of those days when the sun still warms you but you begin to shiver the moment it sets. On that day I was jogging along, enjoying the warmth of the last rays of sunshine when I suddenly felt an inner prompting to return to a particular spot in the woods that I had already passed. I fought with this urge. I had exhausted myself jogging and was not particularly interested in backtracking. The prompting returned. I had learned to listen to these subtle messages, so I gave in, however reluctantly. The spot was a knoll in the woods overlooking a short ravine. When I arrived at the knoll, I was sweaty and tired, and the sun was just beginning to set. I would be cold and shivering within minutes. I stood there and felt rather silly. Then suddenly a large owl came swooping up from the bottom of the ravine, her eyes aimed at me. I held my breath. She perched on a branch about ten feet away and continued to hold eye contact. I stood motionless, pretending to be a tree, which, from the owl's perspective, might have been a silly attempt. I did not want to scare her away. She was beautiful, and she seemed to be checking me out. Slowly, however, the sweat from my forehead dripped into my eyes. It burned. I knew I had to wipe my eyes. Despite all my efforts to resist the motion, I finally gave in, certain I would lose my winged companion. I wiped my eyes, and shivering, I pulled the hood from my sweatshirt over my head. The owl did not seem to mind. Contrary to what I had expected, she began to clean under her wings. Then she turned and showed me her back. Every once in a while, she rotated her head in my direction as only an owl can. It was as if she wanted to make sure I was watching. She performed this little dance within arm's reach from where I stood despite my moving around to keep warm. I could see every detail of her beautiful feathery gown, the intricacy of her facial feathers, her large beak, her incredible strong talons, and her penetrating eyes. Finally she turned fully in my direction again and looked long and deeply into my eyes. Her large and very dark eyes seemed incredibly human. Holding her gaze, I suddenly felt myself engulfed in deep love and serenity. I was stunned by the emotions I felt. The owl and I seemed to blend as beings and become one in that moment. This oneness had an infinite quality. It could not be disturbed or altered. It belonged to a dimension outside opinion or judgment. It had a quality of peace so strong I immediately knew that nothing of this world could affect it. No matter what tragedy or circumstance occurred, this peace was ultimately so much more real. It was eternal.

While we were holding eye contact, her eyes began to remind me of someone, but I couldn't remember who at first. And then suddenly I knew. These were the same large, dark, and loving eyes of a dear friend I called Cousin Gloria, though I was not related to her. A few weeks before, there had been a gathering, and I had had a chance to visit with her. She was in the final stages of cancer, and I was sure it would be the last time I would see her. Not many words were spoken between us during that visit. But when I gave her a good-bye hug, my curious self got the better of me, and I wanted very much to ask her to give me a message from the other side after her passing. Humbled by her circumstances, however, and respectful of her journey ahead, I did not think it was my place to ask for favors. So I left it at the thought, while I felt a little bit ashamed of my ever-so-curious self. All I managed to do was look into her dark, large, and loving eyes for what seemed a long time. Then we parted. Unmistakably, the eyes now looking at me intently from the branch just a few feet away, were the same eyes. The moment I had the thought of recognition, the owl lifted off the branch and swooped back into the woods, out of sight.

As soon as I returned home, I called Cousin Gloria's family and found that she had died that same afternoon. When I shared what I had experienced in the woods, I learned to my surprise that Cousin Gloria had a love for owls and had collected many owl-related trinkets.

The memory of my owl encounter and Cousin Gloria's passing had brought back strong feelings as I passed cage after cage filled with colorful domestic bird varieties. Had Cousin Gloria really heard my silent request during our parting and given me a sign from the other side with the help of the owl?

I believe that messages from the other side are gifts. They don't just cause incredible feelings of joy but also bring us deep peace. Animals often serve as messengers between those who have parted and those of us who still linger here. But what would it take to *truly* know without suspecting, guessing, or maybe hoping that life indeed goes on? Sure, near-death survivors tell stories of wonderful heavens and beautiful beings, but with a doubting Thomas like myself, only personal experience would convince me with certainty that life indeed went on beyond this earthly struggle.

When I left the poultry barns behind and crossed the fairgrounds in the direction of the flower halls, I remembered Amélie. She was a beautiful French-Canadian lady in her midsixties. She was petite and always stylishly dressed, and she was my neighbor Randy's girlfriend. Amélie was known for spending hours on her hair every day, styling it into blond ripples and then firmly securing it with enormous amounts of hairspray. I mostly saw her smoking cigarettes outside the house as I drove in or out on the dirt road we shared. One day I noticed that her smoking session was followed by a coughing fit. As the weeks went on, her coughing episodes lasted longer and sounded worse. Concerned, I spoke with Randy, and he ruefully told me that Amélie refused to see a doctor. A few days after that conversation, I woke in the middle of the night to see ambulance lights flashing through the trees from the direction of my neighbor's house. I knew that it was there for Amélie. I was relieved she would finally receive the help that she did not want but definitely needed.

I returned home from work a couple of nights later, and as I always did, I passed by my neighbor's house. The curve in our shared road allowed me to see directly into their kitchen through a large window. Amélie always sat in the same chair, which was visible for a fleeting moment from the road. And to my surprise, I saw her sitting in her chair, all styled up as usual, her hair perfectly done, talking very animatedly to someone out of view. I was so delighted to see her that I actually stopped my car, turned off the engine, and sat for a few minutes, just watching her. She looked energetic and well, and again I was enjoying her elaborate hairdo, which had been done to perfection. After a while I started the car and continued up the road to my cabin, happy about Amélie's fast recovery.

The next day I saw Randy. I told him that I had seen the ambulance and how happy I was that Amélie was back home so soon, obviously recovered and well. He gave me a puzzled look, and then somewhat perplexed, he informed me that Amélie had actually passed away the night the ambulance had picked her up. Surprised about this news, and not usually a person to share such experiences, I found myself in a bit of an uncomfortable situation with my neighbor. Randy, on the other hand, did not know what to make of me or my story. In true Vermont style, the conversation drifted into acceptable silence as he uttered a final, "Yup."

Deep in thought about Amélie's sudden death, I strolled back to my cabin. There was a smile on my face, however, as I walked up the hill, grateful to Amélie for allowing me a glimpse of her real self and her fancy hairdo two days after her passing. Yes, life *does* indeed go on.

While reminiscing about Amélie, I had arrived at the flower halls. I enjoyed the sounds of the fair, which seemed to increase in direct relation to the advancing hours of the night. Walking through these halls was always an adventure. If you ever wonder what Vermonters do during endlessly long winter nights, the flower halls with their many exhibitions of arts and crafts give away their secrets. Indeed, there are astonishing talents hidden behind those curly beards and long braids. Each year beautifully hand-sewn quilts hang from the walls next to exquisite woodcarvings and paintings, and proud and talented cooks exhibit an array of homemade pies. In the vegetable section, one can find the tallest sunflower, heaviest pumpkin, reddest tomato, greenest bean, largest potato, and many more vegetables and flowers, each carefully judged and crowned for its particular quality. Despite the rough climate, long winters, and early and late frosts, Vermonters manage to coax plants from the soil that make your heart sing.

Homegrown sunflower
Photo: Nick Goldsmith

This year's exhibit was as diverse and inspiring as always. My curiosity satisfied, I left the flower halls. The night sky was filled with blinking lights and screams of excitement and terror coming from the direction of the rides. While rides are fun for those with strong stomachs, I prefer the nostalgic and much slower-paced Ferris wheel. I decided to take a ride to enjoy the activity of the fair from a bird's-eye perspective. High up in the air overlooking the fairgrounds, I smelled a myriad of delicious flavors that reminded me of my love for fair food. When my gondola made it back to the ground, I could no longer resist. Hungry, I first enjoyed the roasted corn drenched in butter and salt, and then I sampled fried dough with a couple of different toppings. I found the apple crisp booth and had a generous helping topped with vanilla ice cream. In spite of the fact that my stomach was already completely full, I treated myself to an overly salted pretzel, an absolute favorite. I enjoyed every bite without the slightest guilt. After all, fair food is only a once-a-year pleasure. Thoroughly in charge of my personal well-being, I had convinced myself that a hearty amount of fair food was a perfect remedy for just about anything. As I did year after year, I arrived at home with a tummy up in arms.

Who Is In Charge Of Our Well-Being?

Despite my failed attempts to assure myself about the health benefits of fair food, I believe we have enormous power over our well-being. We are much more in charge of what happens to us than it appears at first sight. As a matter of fact, I dare speculate that *we are the rulers of our existence.* In the past such a bold statement could have gotten its messenger burned at the stake.

From the world of quantum physics, we learn that all possibilities already exist and that we actually influence that which we make the focus of our attention. This *observer effect* was well demonstrated through the double-slit experiment. It seems that matter changes its behavior in response to observation. Observation occurs simultaneously with thought, and I ask myself, *Since we influence everything we focus our thoughts on, can we increase the well-being of our cells and so improve the quality of our existence by commanding and controlling our thoughts?*

The trillions of cells within our bodies are indeed faithful workers and ready to listen to our thoughts and commands, explains Bruce Lipton, stem cell biologist and leader in the field of new biology. Lipton discovered that the mind is not solely located in the brain but is distributed throughout the whole body. Each of our cells, explains Lipton, has an individual brain within its cell membrane, and it is programmable. Previously it was believed that genes controlled the cell's behavior, but Lipton discovered that each cell's behavior and genetic activity were in fact the cell's interpretation of environmental signals.

The human genome project determined that we humans have roughly twenty-five thousand genes. (This was a big disappointment to the scientific community, as we had expected to be more interesting.) We share 98.5 percent of our genes with those of chimpanzees, and 57 percent of our genes are shared with—believe it or not—a cabbage. Don't like worms? Well, we share 50 percent of our genes with them. You are in luck if you like bananas, as they are our genetic cousins with a genetic match of 30 percent. Formerly we believed that the genes we are born with make us who we are, that we—fortunately or sometimes unfortunately— inherit our genetic makeup from our parents and try to make the best of it. However, recent scientific discoveries have taught that although we all share 99.9 percent of the same twenty-five thousand genes, it is *after* birth that we begin to switch them on and off in response to our cells' interpretation of different environmental signals.

During Lipton's stem cell research, he took one single cell and divided it into two identical cells. Then he continued the cell-splitting process with these two cells until he had thousands of identical cells, all stemming from that one original cell. He then separated them into different vials and watched. With amazement he discovered that one vial would produce fat cells, another muscle cells, and yet another bone cells. The cells were not taking their cue from the genetic code within. Otherwise they all would have developed in the exact same way. The information to develop into different kinds of cells came from somewhere else.

Lipton concluded that our cells are ready to receive and fulfill commands from fellow cells and from the big guy, namely our mind. This means that it is ultimately not the brain that is in charge. How can that be? Isn't it the brain that allows us to function?

There are actually numerous cases in medical literature that describe individuals without brains leading normal and functional lives. John Lorber (1915–1996), a British neurologist, conducted a long series of systematic scans of patients suffering from a condition called hydrocephalus, characterized by abnormal buildup of cerebrospinal fluid in the brain. As a result of hydrocephalus, some patients do not show any evidence of possessing a cerebral cortex. They possess instead a thin layer of mantle, only a millimeter thick. The rest of the cranium is filled with cerebrospinal fluid. Despite this condition, some of the patients Lorber studied led successful and productive lives with IQs greater than a hundred. The information about how to function could not have come from the brain (the cerebral cortex) in these patients.

If, in the absence of a brain, the mind uses signals from the environment and forwards them to the many little brains within each cell membrane of our body, what then runs the mind? Originally our cells were programmed to work in absolute harmony and perfection with each other and to operate without any limitations. Over the course of human history, we have adopted limiting beliefs. These beliefs are so deeply ingrained within our cellular memory that we no longer recognize them as *beliefs* but rather accept them without doubt as *facts*. These beliefs have reprogrammed our cells over time to a point where we experience disease and decay as inevitable parts of human existence. Beliefs are attitudes that govern our lives. Henry Ford once said, "If you believe you can or if you believe you can't, you're right."

It's easy to check this by looking at our own lives. What is it that has driven us based on beliefs and consequently shaped our attitudes and behaviors? Don't we refrain from singing because we believe we do not have a good enough voice? Have parents or teachers removed hope by programming us to believe we are limited or powerless? Do we give up because we have been diagnosed with a disease that has a statistically bleak outlook? Master St. Germain taught, "Where your thoughts are, there you are. What your thoughts are upon, that you *become*." If we can learn to control our thoughts, can we reshape our beliefs, affect our well-being, and hence increase the quality of our lives?

I realized that I needed to have cells clean of faulty cellular memories and beliefs if I wanted to move forward on my personal journey. Faulty beliefs firmly ingrained in my mind would only keep me walking in circles, repeating the same thoughts, feelings, words, and actions over and over again, all the while hoping for a new daybreak. The saying attributed to Albert Einstein, namely that the definition of insanity is doing the same thing over and over again and expecting different results, rang in my mind. Faulty beliefs keep us from living at our full potential. We are all incredible beings that are capable beyond imagination. To be freed from faulty beliefs and self-destructive attitudes will allow our potential to blossom.

Subconscious Mind And Faulty Beliefs

Our conscious mind is capable of analyzing and rationalizing. Our subconscious mind, on the other hand, does not bother with these tasks. We absorb information— whether true or not—into our subconscious mind as irrevocable truths. Unaware, faulty beliefs infiltrate our subconscious mind and begin to shape our attitudes and consequently our lives.

Changing faulty beliefs is possible, however. Aware of our enormous potential, Rhonda Byrne, creator of the movie *The Secret* and author of the book of the same title, successfully used her mind to change the seemingly impossible. Like the rest of us, she believed eyesight diminishes with age. It was not a conscious belief but a so-called fact that society and its massive morphic field teach. Once Byrne was aware that she had fully bought into this belief, she immediately set out to change her thinking. She imagined herself seeing clearly without the help of reading glasses and enjoying perfect eyesight as she had when she was in her twenties. She used her mind to imagine reading in dark places with ease—in restaurants, on planes, on computer screens—and she felt excitement and gratitude for having clear vision. It took just three days, and her eyesight was completely restored. The feat was particularly impressive, especially since the fact that eyesight diminishes after the age of about forty is common knowledge, a morphic field of enormous proportion.

It does not require much to reach and affect our subconscious mind. The lightest and subtlest suggestions are readily welcomed and quickly integrated into our belief system.

On May 25, 1950, a sixteen-year-old man was wheeled into the operating room where Dr. Albert A. Mason, a skilled anesthetist at the Queen Victoria Hospital located in East Grinstead, England, was working. The hospital was known worldwide at the time for its expertise in plastic surgery. The patient suffered from a severe skin condition that covered his entire body with, it appeared to Dr. Mason, millions of black warts. The young patient could hardly move without causing his skin to crack and ooze. A team of plastic surgeons led by Sir Archibald McIndoe attempted to transplant skin from the man's chest to his hands in the hopes that at some point he could use at least his hands for manual labor. They attempted the transplant twice without success.

Sir Archibald McIndoe declared that there was nothing else that could be done. However, Dr. Mason, twenty-five years old at the time and also a skilled hypnotherapist, had another idea. He had been successful in using hypnosis to remove warts. He saw no problem attempting to remove millions of warts applying the same method. He innocently suggested that Sir Archibald McIndoe give hypnosis a try. Already disappointed by his failure and put off by this young doctor's bold suggestion, Sir Archibald McIndoe stormed out of the examination room, cynically suggesting that Dr. Mason should go right ahead and give hypnosis a try.

Mason proceeded with hypnosis, addressing the patient's subconscious mind. Five days after the first session, the skin on the patient's left arm began to heal. Rather pleased with the results, Dr. Mason was eager to show Sir Archibald McIndoe that warts could indeed be removed rather easily with the use of hypnosis. He immediately showed the young man to the surgeon. Shocked by the results, McIndoe informed Mason that the patient was not suffering from a case of warts but rather *congenital ichthyosiform erythrodermia of Brocq*, a rare and incurable skin disease.

It was physiologically impossible for the skin to renew itself because a person with this disease lacked the oil-forming glands that would enable the process. Stunned by this news, Mason was short of an explanation as to how the healing could have taken place.

The unusual case was brought to the Royal Society of Medicine and was documented in the *British Medical Journal*. It caused quite a stir, demanding new attention to the role of the subconscious mind in the healing process. Mason proceeded with his patient and was able to clear about half of the skin on the legs and feet and about 95 percent on the arms and hands. No relapse occurred, and the young man eventually was able to learn a profession and live a normal life.

Soon after his successful case was published, the phone began to ring, and people from all over the world asked to be cured of this terrible and debilitating skin condition. In all, Mason tackled eight more cases of the same rare disease in the years following his initial success. In 1961, however, he announced via the *British Medical Journal* that in every one of those cases his attempts to cure were a complete failure. Not once was he able to duplicate his original success.

As a result, Mason quit his job as an anesthetist, went back to school, and became a psychiatrist, exploring the inner world of the mind and the subconscious. Thirty years later Mason was still mystified by his experience. He concluded that literally anything could be done. To accomplish profound change, however, something equally profound must take place.

In Mason's case, the equally profound that took place was a change in the power of belief. When he first attempted a cure by hypnosis, he was convinced he was dealing with a severe case of warts. He had been successfully healing warts and had no reason to doubt his abilities. Once Sir Archibald McIndoe informed him that the disease was incurable, the information infiltrated Mason's subconscious mind and belief system. No longer was he free to perform without doubt. Nothing had changed—that is, except for the fact that new and crucial pieces of information had entered Mason's subconscious mind.

Once I realized how many deeply ingrained but faulty beliefs affect my mind and consequently my life, I wanted very much to eradicate them. I wanted to make sure I was living at my fullest potential—or at least inch a little closer to it. But I was nicely programmed to believe that we get sick if we don't eat healthy food or that we will certainly die if we don't eat at all. I was programmed to believe that we need a proper education to achieve anything substantial in life, that we are doomed should we not have a fat 401(k) account and establish security in life. I had strong, unshakable beliefs about aging and dying. Everyone ages and dies, right? These were strong beliefs I considered as absolute facts, deeply ingrained over many lifetimes, so deeply rooted that even attempting to think the opposite seemed ridiculous. These were beliefs with monstrous morphic fields.

To step outside of a morphic field, I had to be super alert to my own thinking. It is thought habits that tie us to morphic fields. To break this pattern, I needed to do something drastic. I signed up for a fire walk.

Walking On Hot Coals

Like any good parents would do, my parents taught me not to touch fire or hot coals. Refusing much of my parents' advice while growing up and consequently learning about life the hard way, I thought *this* advice was good actually. Touching hot coals will result in a burn. I heat my house with a woodstove, and every now and then when a red, glowing coal falls out while I'm loading the stove, I quickly grab it with my fingers and toss it back inside the firebox. I do it as speedy as the wind because I can feel its heat, and I still often get burned a little. Hot coals burn human flesh. It's a fact, and yes, a belief with a huge morphic field. Putting all my body weight on hot coals when I'm barefoot and then walking on them sounded like a perfect and exciting way to test the possibility of a new horizon. What if I could actually walk on hot coals? What else that I had previously considered impossible could I do? I tried to invite a friend to come with me, but she quickly suggested learning to walk on water first. Obviously my friend is smarter than I am. Still I went.

It was not easy to find a fire walk in the area I live in. I was lucky, however, as one was scheduled in the neighboring state New Hampshire, a two-hour drive from my home. While I drove to the event, I had plenty of time to imagine myself walking on hot coals. It did not work. The idea of walking barefoot over hot coals simply did not conform to what I knew and believed in. It was a perfect way to test whether deeply ingrained beliefs truly could be altered. And since I had never heard of anyone getting seriously injured or dying during a fire walk, I was full of curiosity and anticipation.

Upon my arrival in the early evening, I found a mixed group of about twenty people of all ages and backgrounds. For most it was the first fire-walk experience. Despite the fact that there are countless arguments about fire walking not being real or being some kind of trick, I can confirm with certainty and personal experience that the coals are indeed very real. We built the fire together shortly after our arrival, each participant putting one log after another deliberately onto the stack until it reached chest height. Once we lit the fire, the flames shot fifteen feet or more into the air, forcing us to step back. While the fire burned down to coals, we spent the next three hours preparing for the big event under the guidance of a skilled leader. The work allowed us to discover what we experienced as our personal limitations or the beliefs that held us back. I was surprised at how many limiting beliefs came to my awareness, some originating back to childhood. I was ready to kick them all.

At one point during the evening, we summarized our limitations into one word and were instructed to write it onto a wooden arrow. On my arrow I wrote the word *security*. We were then instructed to lean the tail end of the arrow against a wooden picture of Ganesha, a Hindu deity symbolizing the "remover of obstacles." The other end of the arrow had a rounded metal tip. The tip was to rest directly against our skin at the bottom of our throat where we have that small, soft, and very tender indentation below the thyroid gland. Our arms were to remain by our sides, not touching the arrow. Then with the emotional and vocal support of all participants, we were to take heart and resolutely step forward into the arrow and break it with the sheer pressure from our throat. This daring move was supposed to help us break through our restricting beliefs.

This is something you would imagine only a group of stupidly drunk college freshmen would attempt. All my life my throat has been a particularly sensitive area for me. I cannot endure anyone or anything touching my throat. This sensation is so extreme that I will avoid whenever possible wearing a scarf in the winter, even though our temperatures in Vermont dip way below freezing. All my turtlenecks have zippers so I can immediately free my throat from any contact the moment I have escaped the cold. Humorously I toy with the idea that at some point in one of my previous lives, I was strangled or hanged. (Knowing my inquisitive mind and my quick tongue, I probably suffered both fates.)

Had I not been so eager to shed my limiting beliefs, I would not have been able to even attempt this arrow-breaking business. But I wanted to be free of my limitations more than anything at that moment. I stepped up when it was my turn and tentatively placed the tip of the arrow against the tender spot in my throat. Alarmingly I felt the point of the arrow, sharp and threatening. I had clear images of stepping forward, the arrow penetrating the skin and exiting at the back of my neck, blood squirting everywhere to the horror of all. I could see myself wrecking this wonderful freeing experience for everyone, causing a liability lawsuit for the group leader and being transported to the emergency room with an arrow stuck through my neck. Finally and perhaps worst of all, I would have to explain the whole thing to my incredulous daughter. But I heard the chanting of the others, felt the excitement rising, and sensed the possibility in what I had thought impossible. I took a deep breath and stepped forward. The arrow split in half with a loud snap just where I had written the word *security*. To my surprise and delight, my throat had remained unscathed. I was intrigued.

I had imagined preparations for the fire walk would result in something of an altered state of consciousness because "in my right mind," I could not imagine myself walking over a bed of hot coals. We had prepared well, had done deep soul work in the yurt, and had accomplished some unlikely feats that boosted our confidence and gave us glimpses of new possibilities, but the moment I stepped outside the yurt and into the dark, I was as solidly grounded as a boulder. I certainly was not in any altered state of mind. Barefooted and dressed in a short skirt, I took one look at the coals. They were glowing menacingly deep red and orange, and had been spread into a three- to four-inch-thick carpet approximately ten feet long. Immediately I thought, *I don't think so.* Yet the chanting continued. The excitement kept rising. The group kept moving, and before I knew it, I stood at the edge of the glowing carpet of red-hot coals.

It was my turn to walk. In the second that I lifted one foot over the coals, my mind split between simultaneous thoughts of alarm and reassurance. Images of a sizzling steak flickered through my imagination, and my nose instinctively searched for the familiar smell of a barbecue. But there were no screams from those who had walked before me. No bodies were rolling in pain on the ground, and my thoughts of reassurance won over fear. I put the foot down ... and walked. I felt the coals, their shape and their heat against the tender skin of my feet. Surprisingly they did not seem to burn like the small pieces did that I often tossed back into the woodstove. I walked across the coals in astonishment. With every step I was more amazed at what I was doing. I did not walk slowly, and I did not run. I crossed the coals at a brisk walk, jumped off the glowing carpet with a squeal of delight only to turn around and do it again. I walked on hot coals seven times that night, one time with a drum in my hand, one time holding hands with another participant. The last time was the slowest walk, as I was giving thanks to the fire and the coals for their teachings. I never got a burn—a fire kiss—as it is called in fire-walk lingo.

My drive home from the fire walk was long, but I did not care. I had so much to contemplate. How was this possible? How could I walk on hot coals and not get burned? Not everyone in our group had enjoyed the same experience. Some folks had suffered a fire kiss strong enough that they were unable to push the pedals in their car on the drive home. The coals were real, yet my feet were absolutely fine. My mind was racing. What other beliefs do I have that keep me from truly being who I am and being able to do what I am actually capable of? How can I rid myself of these beliefs, and will I be able to stay clear of the enormous societal morphic fields that could hold me back? After all, I *can* walk on hot coals!

I decided very consciously not to buy into what I began to recognize as false beliefs and continued to watch my thoughts keenly. I realized, however, that I was not only struggling with my own false beliefs, but by living amongst other people who accept many beliefs as facts and live by them daily, I was also subject to their belief systems. Merely by being in the presence of someone, I would exchange atoms with that person. I could not separate myself from my world. I was entangled with everyone and everything that exists.

Connectedness, Interconnectedness, and Entanglement

We got glimpses into this reality of ultimate connectedness or entanglement in 2008, when physicists in Switzerland at the University of Geneva took two entangled photons and managed to separate them by eighteen kilometers. They then messed with one photon and observed that its counterpart, separated by considerable distance, showed the same response at the exact same time. The physicists tried the experiment over and over again. The photons still seemed connected and communicating in a mysterious way. The physicists calculated that if the photons were in fact communicating with each other, the communication would have had to travel more than one hundred thousand times faster than the speed of light.

Simplified, photons have energy. All mass is essentially made up of energy, which ultimately will return to light one day. Mass includes humans as well. Hence, it makes sense that we, essentially light beings, are connected and influence one another consciously or subconsciously, even separated by thousands of miles or possibly lifetimes. In fact, it seems that we are connected not only to other human beings but also to animals, plants, and our earth, and it appears we are connected even to the planets of the universe. Many religious, indigenous, and shamanic traditions already know about this connectedness.

In his book *The Isaiah Effect*, Gregg Braden makes reference to the ancient 2,500-year-old writings of the Dead Sea Scrolls. From the Dead Sea Scrolls, Braden learned that the Essenes already understood connectedness. They believed that man's spirit was created from the heavenly father and that man's body was created from the body of the earthly mother. In their own language more than two millennia ago, the Essenes explained that humanity was one with the heavens and the earth. Twenty-five hundred years later, science is inching closer to proving them right.

Schumann Resonances

That the moon has an effect on humans and on the earth is obvious. It gently rocks our tides back and forth and much less gently throws our emotional balance off kilter during full moons. If you are a woman, you are particularly aware of and often in sync with the moon's cycles. The sun, however, has a strong effect on us as well. Dr. Winfried Schumann, a German physicist, discovered in 1952 what was later named the Schumann resonances. Schumann resonances are the measurements of the electrical tension between the earth and the ionosphere. The ionosphere is a conductive plasma layer surrounding our planet that is caused by radiation from the sun. The ionosphere is positively charged. The earth's surface carries a negative charge. In between is a cavity of nonconducting air that causes the electrical tensions. The lowest frequency of Schumann resonances is measured at a frequency of approximately 7.83 Hz, which is surprisingly similar to the frequency of human brain waves. Struck by this similarity, scientists took the leap and investigated whether solar activity affecting the ionosphere could have an influence on human health and behavior.

Through the Global Coherence Initiative of the HeartMath Institute, an institution located in Boulder Creek, California, whose technology is used by tens of thousands of people around the world today, ultrasensitive magnetic field detectors measure the Schumann resonances. These detectors are located around the globe and accumulate data without interruption. With their help, the Global Coherence Initiative was able to demonstrate that increased solar activity, especially geomagnetic storms, strongly relate to adverse human health effects. Annette Deyhle, a member of the Global Coherence Initiative (GCI) research team, reported that scientific studies have shown that periods of solar and geomagnetic activity are followed by a number of human ailments. Scientist have noted an increase in depression, fatigue, suicides, migraine attacks, significant changes in blood pressure, an increase in mortality rates from strokes and heart attacks, and even a reduction in birthrates.

Deyhle reported that increased solar activity not only affects human health and behavior but also seems to influence social unrest, revolutions, and war. Russian scientist A. L. Tchijevsky, who studies solar cycles and human behavior, discovered that over a span of more than two millennia of recorded history, eighty percent of the most significant events on earth caused by humans occurred during the five years around peak sunspot activity. To come to this conclusion, Tchijevsky compiled the history of seventy-two countries from 500 BC to AD 1922. Other scientists took Tchijevsky's compilation forward to the year 1985 and confirmed the relationship between solar activity and violence. Solar sunspots are named by numbers and have approximately an eleven-year cycle. Solar cycle 22 peaked sharply as Iraq invaded Kuwait, and solar cycle 23 peaked dramatically at the time of the 9/11 attacks on the World Trade Centers. We are currently in the midst of solar cycle 24.

Deyhle also pointed out that increased solar activity is not just an adverse time for human health and the cause for increased social unrest, but it gives rise to human excellence as well. Scientists who have researched the correlation between social unrest, terrorist attacks, and revolutions with times of increased solar activity discovered that these times correlate with a rise in human creativity and productivity in the fields of science, the arts, and architecture. It appears these unruly solar activities may help unleash some of humankind's enormous potential.

This mysterious interconnectedness exists between everything and anything, beginning with quantum particles like photons and extending to minerals, plants, animals, people, distant stars, planets, and even the sun of our solar system. It will be exciting to witness future discoveries and new evidence of connectedness and entanglement. Maybe evidence will be found in destinations beyond our solar system, beyond our galaxy, in other galaxies of our universe, and someday maybe even beyond our own universe.

CHAKRAS: ENERGY TRANSFORMERS

At the beginning of my 365-day journey while I was contemplating exactly how I was going to nourish myself with prana, I had an idea of dividing the journey into 365 meals. I envisioned a personal chef whom I imagined to be my nutritional head honcho.

I saw my head honcho as a jolly fellow who was as round as he was tall, a man with a big smile and rosy cheeks. He was stirring a huge cauldron containing my daily load of delicious nutrients. As my personal chef, he had been doing this for eons, making sure I received what I needed for a healthy existence. This would include plenty of proteins, carbohydrates, vitamins, minerals, and electrolytes, as well as things I did not even know of.

My head honcho was very loyal. He always did his best and enjoyed his work. He was proud of his daily contribution. And he should have been by all means. He had nourished me in this lifetime alone for several decades already. On the first day of my journey, I had a little mental conversation with him. I thanked him for his loyalty and his wonderful work. Then I informed him that from now on we would change our routine a little bit. Every day starting with the first day of my journey, he would add a shake from an imaginary spice shaker that was filled with sparkling prana to the mix. The first day my head honcho would add only one shake. On the second day, he would add two shakes, and on the third day, he would add three and so on, slowly getting me used to a higher and higher dose of prana. I had learned that prana was ever-abundantly available, so the magic prana shaker would always be full. On the last day of our contract, he would add 365 shakes, enough to sustain me on prana alone if need be. That was our agreement.

The first day was funny. Head honcho looked at me like I had asked him to spoil his lovely culinary creation. I assured him that it would be just fine and that he might even enjoy this special addition to the mix. We both witnessed his very first shake. Prana sprinkled out of the shaker like fresh snow in the morning sun. Little sparkles mixed into a healthy multicolored mass of nutrients. He stirred energetically, and we discovered that the mix had the slightest glow. Something new was definitely in the pot.

Every day since, together we have been adding one additional shake per day. At day forty-nine of the journey, the mix had a distinct glow, and my head honcho was quite enchanted with the idea. Sometimes, after he added the proper amount of prana into the cauldron, he would shake some on top of his head. Snowflakes of prana would sparkle all over him. We both would laugh. There was plenty for all.

Day forty-nine was also an auspicious day. I knew it the moment I awoke and looked at my notepad, where I kept a record of each day of this adventure. Day forty-nine meant forty-nine shakes of prana for my body from my lovely and faithful head honcho. I had come to an interesting milestone on this journey. Seven, of course, goes seven times into forty-nine. I realized that it was possible to divide the forty-nine shakes of prana into seven shakes for each of the seven major chakras we have in our body. I understood that they in turn could then nourish my glandular system, which then again could nourish my entire physical body and beyond. Here was a new and purposeful way of distributing prana throughout my body, reaching each and every cell. This was exciting. Eureka! I felt empowered. I had no idea at this point how significant this daily ritual would become for the later part of my journey.

Chakra is the Sanskrit word for *wheel*. In her work *Living with Your Light Turned On*, Virginia Smith teaches that chakras are spinning vortexes of energy that absorb, metabolize, and distribute life-sustaining energy (prana) throughout our cellular structure. There are many more energy centers in our body, but the seven major chakras are the energy headquarters. They are vertically aligned along our spinal cord, and they have been a focus in philosophies and old traditions for spiritual growth, healing, insight, and enlightenment. As our awareness increases, our chakras will open and allow us to metabolize and handle greater amounts of prana.

Each major chakra has a different color, says Smith. When a chakra functions at optimum level, its color will be more intense and vibrant. When we get exhausted, Smith explains, our muscles will signal our brain to draw energy from its reserves, which in return stimulates our chakras to regulate and distribute this energy where needed throughout the body. Our degree of insight, awareness, and enlightenment is dependent on the amount of prana our chakras can absorb. Prana sustains us, says Smith, even if we do not realize this on a conscious level. It is the substance that causes our chakras to spin. The more energy we can absorb, the higher the velocity at which the chakras spin. If the chakras are only partially opened (or even closed as a result of negativity we have produced), energy cannot flow freely. This will result in energy blocks and imbalances that eventually will cause physical, emotional, or mental disease. The quality of our thoughts, feelings, and memories directly determine the speed and direction at which our chakras spin.

The chakras can be easily envisioned as light centers, orbs, or discs, rotating along our spinal cord. When they emanate light at their highest potential, they can create a disc-like glow around the body. Throughout history the sometimes-visible glow of the crown chakra has been painted in the form of a halo on saints.

＊

When I first learned about these energy centers and started to focus on them, I tuned in with my eyes closed and began to literally see and feel them. To my horror, my sacral chakra, also called the second root chakra, looked more like a mushroom than a disk. It appeared spongy and warped and rotated counterclockwise. It kept shrinking every time I checked in on it. Its color was yellowish brown, not orange as it was supposed to be. I did not think that was a very good sign. I began consciously infusing it with light, which I drew in through my crown chakra, and with love from my heart chakra. Both these chakras seemed healthy.

After I worked with the sacral chakra for a while—I checked in daily and supported it energetically—against my expectation, the chakra began to shrink even more! One night during a dance, I felt inclined to check in on the condition of my chakras. To my utter astonishment and grave concern, the sacral chakra had shrunk to an alarming fraction of its original self. It appeared as though the unsightly shaped chakra was eating itself. I was disturbed, bordering on panic while outwardly presenting a smile and following the rhythm of the music. I was not sure if I could even exist without one of the seven major chakras. Had this ever happened to anyone before? I continued to dance, trying to enjoy myself. I checked in a little later. The chakra had become even smaller, and then it seemed to disappear entirely. This was not the goal I had had in mind when I had begun my chakra-cleansing routine. I took heart, however, and summoned all the courage and trust I could muster. I knew I needed to trust the process of this journey, no matter how it would unfold. I felt guided and was aware that as I took baby steps along this path, I would wander into unfamiliar territory. And unfamiliar it was indeed. But just when I thought I would be the only person on this globe kicking up my heels and dancing with only six major chakras, I noticed the smallest hint of color emanating from my spinal cord where the old chakra used to be. The chakra literally regrew out of the spinal cord like a budding flower. I watched it grow over the days following the dance, and it unfolded into a colorful wheel. It is now a strong disk emanating a beautiful tricolored light.

After day forty-nine of my journey, I proceeded to distribute the daily pranic meals specifically to the seven major chakras. On day forty-nine, each chakra received seven shakes of prana (purest light energy) in addition to my head honcho's nutritional concoction. On day fifty, each chakra received again seven shakes, but one chakra received eight. In this way I continued to spread the pranic meals every day until, by the end of my 365-day journey, each chakra would receive fifty-two shakes, except for one which would receive fifty-three. My scrap paper would help me keep track of this number business.

Distributing prana to each chakra caused me to focus on them on a daily basis. I began to appreciate their individual shades of color and their various sizes and shapes, and I watched them spin, sometimes all in different directions. As the days went by, I noticed slight changes. My chakras began to radiate more vibrantly, align themselves at times in a vertical line along the spine, and spin, however rarely, in unison. I really had no idea why I was doing this the way I was doing it. But I knew it was important because I recognized that amongst other benefits prana would also nourish, rejuvenate, and heal my chakras.

∗

It was hard to believe that only a couple of months had passed since the beginning of my journey. I began to understand that we have access to information stored in morphic fields, information that can speed up and aid us along our personal, evolutionary journey. I realized that our thoughts are directed by the beliefs we hold dear. We create these beliefs through our interpretation of the signals we receive from our environment. Depending on our interpretation, false beliefs may become facts and hence govern our lives. Through connections, interconnections, and entanglements, we are influenced not just by our immediate surroundings but by all and everything that exists, even the stars and planets of our galaxy. I began to understand that our environment stimulates our genes. We turn genes on or off depending on how we perceive and process events. It is not the cerebral cortex alone that governs our body but the mind, which is capable of creating, destroying, overriding, and redirecting anything. The mind sends out thought signals to trillions of our cells. Cell membranes, each equipped with their own brains, execute the commands. I learned that negative thoughts and painful memories keep our chakras from spinning at their highest velocity, hold our vibrations at low levels, prevent us from absorbing light energy, and inhibit us from living at our highest potential. I had begun a conscious process of cleansing myself of such negativity with the prospect of eventually being able to absorb more light energy. It was a promising start.

Beginning Of Hibernation

The appearance of Vermont had changed. Glorious fall had come to an end. Temperatures had dropped, and the beautifully colored leaves had fallen, covering the ground in a soft blanket. Left behind were naked trees against gray, foggy landscapes. In its own way, this stick season, as this precursor to winter is called among locals, has its own beauty and serenity. It is also one of the favorite seasons of many Vermonters—the impatiently awaited hunting season.

In Vermont, hunting tradition is alive and well. Deer hunting as a way to fill the family's freezer is an economic reality for many. The woods in November are my favorite place to roam, and it took a while to become accustomed to the idea that while I was hiking in the forest, I could come across not just adults in their hunter plaid and orange but also their identically clad children armed with their own rifles. I was so intrigued by this and, I admit, a bit frightened that I wore my own orange hat so that hunters could see me from afar and hopefully distinguish me from a turkey or a buck. I also decided to attend the hunters' education course and get my own hunting license. In this way I figured I would learn what they knew and how they went about their sport. I could then plot my personal defense and survival strategy. It was a memorable experience. Of course, the kids at the hunter education course had the benefit of having accompanied their fathers (and on occasion mothers) to hunting camp prior to attending the course. They knew the sport well and were familiar with the use of a rifle and ammunition. They understood hunting methods from experience, and they proved themselves to be eager and attentive learners. My respect for these youngsters—mostly boys but also some girls—grew, as I was deeply impressed by what we all had to learn in order to pass the rigorous test. Although I enjoyed target shooting and was comfortable blowing skeet out of the sky with a shotgun, I was, to their great amusement, the first vegetarian to attend the hunter's education course.

There are many different hunting seasons in fall. But the annual sixteen-day rifle deer-hunting season is the most favored. It is a time when workmen suddenly disappear. You may think you had your electrician or plumber all lined up only to come to realize that they are nowhere to be found. Tracking down a buck can take days, and many persistent hunters do not shy away from following the tracks up and down the hills and mountains of Vermont until they reach their prey.

Years ago a friend's great-uncle was on the way to his own wedding when a bear happened to cross the road in front of him. Dressed in wedding clothes and ready to tie the knot, he jumped off the wagon, rifle in hand, and pursued the bear. He disappeared for two weeks before he returned with the hide as a wedding gift for his patiently waiting bride.

Of course, accidents happen as well. There was an incident when a bow hunter accidentally shot a logger off his tractor. Apparently he had mistaken the logger for a turkey. Later during the investigation, it was discovered that the "turkey" coincidentally had had a romantic relationship with the bow hunter's wife.

Often the first snow falls during hunting season, which gives special charm to the surroundings and suddenly reveals all the comings and goings of the animal world. Cornstalks, cut short by harvesting machines, show their beautiful and wavy growing patterns—dark reeds standing in sharp contrast against white snow. This is the time for putting away tools and tidying up barns and sheds while the last flocks of Canada Geese head south in elegant V-shape formations. The days have become significantly shorter. Woodstoves have been working for weeks and will do so for months to come. For Vermonters it is the time to finally tuck in for the long cold season ahead. Hibernation has begun.

PART III

WINTER

TRUST AND SURRENDER

Winter in Vermont is relentlessly long and has a repertoire that will leave you speechless. It will snow, and if you are a skier like me, that's a wonderful thing. But don't think you can wait even one day to finish a project before you enjoy that lovely powder. The ice-cold northern winds will set in before the last snowflake has fallen and pack the beautiful fluff into a hard, unskiable surface. And while you are pursuing your passion in the backcountry, Mr. Winter is busy burying your house and driveway, so you will have ample work to do upon your return.

The beautiful powder is often followed by a rainstorm. And rain in winter is not only messy but typically chased by a deep freeze. These bitter-cold days of ice are the days when cars will not start and water refuses to come out of the faucet. Everything slows to a crawl and not much gets accomplished. Vermonters daring to venture outside are hunched over, dressed in wool hats and plaid jackets, and shuffle along in big insulated boots. Those of us choosing to stay inside will snuggle closer to the woodstove with a cup of hot cocoa, dreaming of enjoying springtime and planting seeds in the garden. That part we love, even when the modern world is finally defeated and the power goes out.

Typical rainstorm following a snowstorm in Vermont
Photo: Isa Oehry

By now my world was covered in several feet of snow. However, I still took my daily lunch walks dressed in warm, insulated boots with knee-high gators. The gators allowed me to walk into the untracked woods where no one else would venture this time of year. My outer layer—a warm hat, thick coat, scarf covering my face, and insulated gloves—was my first defense. Hidden and underneath my regular winter clothing, I wore what I call my "love-killers," the very unsexy and unsightly long underwear without which one cannot survive a winter in Vermont.

This daily walk created a refuge for me. When work would take my focus off my journey, I could reconnect during my lunch walk. My mind would instantly become peaceful when my eyes fell upon a small mound of snow resting on a hemlock branch. Here, I contemplated my journey. I was astounded at what had transpired so far. Doors had opened, and insights had flooded my consciousness during the day and my subconscious mind during vivid dreams at night. The search for the legendary wisdom of prana had been the catalyst to start me on an amazing journey of discovery. These contemplations helped me to develop trust. I sensed that everything I needed would be supplied if there was sincere effort on my part, and I knew that I was guided.

I decided that rather than doubting and often fighting what was taking place in my life, I would instead try to flow with circumstances and surrender to the process. And believe me, surrendering was not exactly my first choice. Years ago I had competed in a sport called telemark skiing. My fellow competitors and I were mostly former alpine ski racers who had turned to telemark skiing because of our love of the backcountry. For several years in a row, I was the women's champion in the Eastern United States, and then I competed in the world championships held in Austria, where I managed to bring home silver and bronze for my country of birth, the Principality of Liechtenstein. You can't be a competitor if you are not a stern and determined fighter. Racing at that level means fierce competition, reckless abandonment of all caution and concern for your body, intense focus, and determination against all odds. Surrendering was not part of my vocabulary. Neither did I find it very attractive at the time. However, once I admitted to myself that I was blessed with limited insight, a marginal understanding of the bigger picture, and a case of total blindness when it came to making wise decisions for my own good, *surrendering* and trusting my guidance seemed a much better choice—at least in theory. It was not going to be an easy transition.

The struggle for survival seemed ingrained in every fiber of my being. Without the fighter in me, I could not have lived in a cabin with a baby, tucked away in the hills of Vermont where I had to learn how to survive in very simple circumstances and on limited resources. All the qualities that had aided me in competing were indispensable during that time of my life. Yet something inside me was begging me to let go. Something was prompting me to move into a new space. I had come to know deep inside where I belonged; however, I was frightened to be there and leave the predictable and *secure* world behind.

Surrendering was harder than I imagined. Despite the lovely snow and the beautiful winter surroundings, my days were suddenly overshadowed by feelings of loss and confusion. I could not remember my goal in life or my purpose. During these days of my journey, I felt lonely and sad. I could not feel my soul. I was lost. I was empty. I decided to surrender. I surrendered to my feelings of loneliness, sadness, and emptiness. And instead of blaming myself, I accepted what I was feeling, and I waited.

Only a couple of weeks later, I snapped out of it as fast as I had fallen into it, renewed, curious, eager, and energized to move forward. When I snapped out of it, I was perhaps a little smarter too. I had not been getting enough quiet time during the holiday season, time alone to contemplate, to connect with my inner world, to reenergize and rejuvenate. Without this quiet time, I shrivel like a flower depleted of light. I made a promise to myself to go about life in a more mindful way.

Kaleidoscope Of Infinite Possibilities

This noble idea of rest did not last long. All good intentions were forgotten with the gift of an unexpected day off from work and sunshine in the forecast. I felt like my old self again, and I craved adventure, high altitude, and maybe a challenge. In addition to sunshine, the weatherman also predicted severe cold temperatures and high winds, but not just any kind of wind. This would be the kind that blows up along the East Coast and then heads far into northern Canada and beyond. Up north, it picks up the frigid air of the Arctic, turns around, and blasts its newly acquired ice-cold spirit through New England on its way out to the ocean. We dread these winds, as they make us cover all skin to protect from frostbite. Ice climbing, one of my favorite pastimes during winter, was not going to be my first choice on such a cold and windy day. It was Mount Moosilauke, one of New Hampshire's proud four-thousand-footers, that was calling my name. Every year I climb this beautiful mountain on foot during the dry seasons and on skis during winter, using skins for the ascent. *Skinning* up a mountain is a wonderful way to keep warm despite brisk temperatures and high winds.

I quickly contacted three strong and adventurous friends, letting them know of my marvelous idea and sending out an invitation. Ernie, a straight shooter who was dependable and easygoing, a good travel companion, and a pleasant climbing partner, thought there was not going to be enough snow to skin up and ski down the mountain safely. (It turned out he was right to a certain extent.) Tommy was older than me, and he was a fabulous athlete who could easily ski circles around those of us younger enthusiasts. He thought it would be too cold and windy. (It turned out he was also right, even underestimating the situation a little.) And sweet and fun Tim was mainly interested in warming

55

his tootsies under my blanket. With no positive responses to my invitation for this adventure, I was on my own.

I set my clock for 4:30 a.m., but I slept in until 5:30. I was headed out by six o'clock, well wrapped in layers of clothing that would allow me to adjust to various altitudes, winds, and temperatures. Carriage Road was the trail of choice, a moderately steep 5.1-mile-long access road leading to a ridgeline below the peak. It was a trail that would offer good skiing, especially at the top, if snow conditions allowed. The sun was just rising as I arrived at the trailhead, wrapping the mountaintop in a beautiful, innocent-looking pink blanket. The gage on my dashboard indicated a temperature well below zero.

I strapped the climbing skins on the skis and started my ascent. Slowly and deliberately I fell into a rhythm, pushing my skis forward step-by-step, carefully avoiding open waterways, and navigating around uncovered rocks. I appreciated the beauty my surroundings offered. To adventure with friends is a special treat, but a solo adventure has a unique and irresistible draw. Where conversation would have taken place, the void could now be filled with keen observation and a quiet mind as well as the birth of new thought. I felt connected with my equipment, the snow, and the mountain, while the roaring wind rocked the trees, snapping frozen branches all around me. I steadily forged on, answering to the call of the summit.

I was following a set of snowshoe tracks maybe a day or two old. These tracks held on to a secret, telling me nothing about their owner. A set of large zigzagging dog tracks, on the other hand, told stories of joy, vitality, exploration, sniffing, and marking. Both sets of tracks made me feel I had company. I was mysteriously connected to those beings, dog and human, who had left these tracks. I remembered the experiment with the entangled photons and what it revealed about connectedness. The dog, the trees, and we ourselves are not unlike photons. If there was a big bang that started all of creation and everything began to exist over time in the various forms and shapes of entangled particles, then indeed we are all of the same origin and interconnected.

The snowshoe and dog tracks suddenly took a wide turn, heading back down the mountain. I had only a set of perfectly straight coyote tracks to follow. I marveled at the precision of the animal's gait. It may as well have been hopping on one foot in a long, straight line. Instinctively, to preserve energy, a coyote will always place its paws in the first track it makes—that is, unless it is running. I took out my camera to snap a photo of the tracks in the fresh, glittering snow. Instantly my batteries died in the frigid cold. But I knew a little warmth would bring them back to life. Quickly I took them out of the camera and stuffed them close to my skin right into the perfect pouch of my bra for a recharge.

Higher up, the scenery changed. The wind increased in strength, and despite the brilliant sunshine, the temperature dropped with each additional foot of altitude gained. My layers of clothing kept me warm, however, and I pushed on. I appreciated my body and enjoyed its loyal obedience to my ever-crazy ideas. I knew I was physically strong, but I also knew I was in some ways weak—a dichotomy. I pondered the realization that I was usually a peaceful person but at times a fierce creature like a tiger. I am very female and soft, yet I am also male and strong. I am educated and ignorant at the same time. I can love and hate, accept and reject. I am a vegetarian with a rifle, a pacifist who can kill. I am proud and yet humble, a teacher and a student. I am a mother and a father, a daughter and a son all in one. I am old, and yet I am young. I am courageous and also afraid, beautiful and ugly. I am a kaleidoscope of infinite possibilities.

Power And Creation Of Memories

Continuing my steady ascent, I remembered that, according to theories of quantum physics, all possibilities already exist at the so-called level of chaos. It is the observer, me, who organizes chaos into personal reality by interpreting events and creating memories. These memories become my beliefs and my reality. In fact, I am the walking image of my personal beliefs.

David Hamilton, pharmaceutical scientist, explains that the recalling of significant experiences, good or bad, will cause our genes to express themselves repeatedly, creating long-lasting memories. This repetition, which we do twenty-four hours a day whether we are awake or asleep, is crucial, says Hamilton, as it causes biological changes, such as the formation of neurons.

None of these memories are lost. In fact, they are stored within our cell membranes, says stem cell biologist Bruce Lipton. He proposes that a single cell membrane has a memory data bank that far exceeds a contemporary silicon chip and records experiences in their minutest detail as well as our reactions to and our beliefs about them. According to Lipton, our immaculate cellular data bank reaches back to our earliest existence.

Researchers at the HeartMath Institute discovered how our memories have a substantial, physiological influence on us. At the institute the researchers took human DNA and placed it in a test tube. Then they instructed the person whose DNA they had captured to hold the test tube and recall traumatic memories. The results showed that the recollection of traumatic memories had physically damaged the DNA in the test tube. The researchers took the same DNA, which was now damaged, and instructed the subject to hold it while recalling beautiful, positive memories. The damaged DNA in the test tube began to repair itself—physiological proof that our memories directly affect our DNA!

I know that I am at times a highly dangerous, even potentially lethal thinker—at least to myself—and at other times I am the best healer. There are more than enough painful memories in my data bank to create an entire collection of new Shakespearian dramas. Continuing my ascent along Carriage Road, I concluded that memories and our thoughts about them are to be taken extremely seriously and should be wrapped with a large label stating, "Fragile–handle with care!"

Lost in thought, while contemplating the significance of creating and recalling memories, I had reached the beginning of the prominent ridgeline of Mount Moosilauke, which was also the end of Carriage Road. Since I had skipped breakfast in the early hours of the day, I was hungry and looking forward to my staple snack of bread, cheese, a hard-boiled egg, and a cup of hot tea. To my surprise, the egg, which I had safely stored in my backpack, had frozen. I poured myself a cup of tea, immersed the egg, and enjoyed my breakfast. Luckily I am never picky about diet on the mountain.

My hunger satisfied and my energy restored, it was time for me to venture out along the ridge trail among the small frozen evergreens. The trees lining the path on both sides of the exposed ridge were covered in a thick layer of rime ice. They looked cold and miserable, forced to stay small and crippled by the never-ending assault of wind and weather at high altitude.

At the end of the ridgeline, I was rewarded with an unobstructed view of Mount Moosilauke's peak, void of vegetation, covered in ice and snow with a lonely summit marker at its peak. The deep blue sky contrasted sharply with the sparkling whiteness of the mountaintop. The wind, even fiercer here, blew snow and ice off the summit, extending a white cloud like a carpet into the sky. I contemplated whether to try to reach the summit. I am not your fragile girl from a country-western song, a hundred pounds soaking wet. I am 140 pounds of Swiss cow bones, as a good friend of mine dared to point out, mostly covered with muscle. I pride myself on "swimming like a rock," needing all my strength to keep from sinking. Today, however, this might come in handy. Of course, I would give the summit a try. I was bundled up under a hooded down jacket, an insulated puffball over a woolen hoody, a vest, an expedition-weight turtleneck, a second turtleneck, and wick shirt over a bra (by this time minus batteries). My bottom layers were pretty much similar. I looked like the Michelin man.

I could see the trail marked with cairns—piles of carefully stacked stones each five to six feet tall—aiding hikers in finding the path in bad weather. The relentless wind at this altitude had blown all snow off the trail leading to the summit, exposing its ice-covered bed of rocks. This was no place for skis. I left them behind, tucked under one of the crippled trees on the ridge, and I began to fight my way on foot. The wind attacked me hard from behind, which kept my face, though completely covered, safe from frostbite for the time being. It got more and more fierce, however, and I had to use all my strength as well as my ski poles to keep from being blown off the trail. Slowly, I managed to work my way up the ice-covered rocks while precariously moving from cairn to cairn and frequently stumbling like an unsteady drunk. Finally, I reached the top and dove behind a pile of rocks maybe three feet tall, the remains of a stone building. I estimated that I was only eight to ten yards away from the peak marker, the official summit. *No place to linger here*, I thought. Quickly I dug out my camera and got it ready. After a summit picture, I would be on my way.

As I emerged from my hiding place, a gust picked me up with ease and slammed me against the stones that secured the summit marker. I heard the clinking of metal against rock—my camera. It had escaped my grip and was landing hard. I knew this was not a life-threatening situation; however, I was keenly aware that if I injured myself, the window of time to escape these elements would be small, and a quick retreat crucial to survival. Pushed against the summit rocks, I was still warm under all my layers of clothing, and I was determined. This was between the wind and me. I remembered my earlier thoughts of the day. Yes, I may be fierce and strong. Now, though, it seemed I was merely a toy for the intense power of this tempest.

I grabbed the camera (which had landed near me between the rocks), jumped up, wrapped my arm around the sign, and turned my face into the wind for just one quick shot. Then the camera died.

Holding on to the summit marker of Mount Moosilauke
Photo: Isa Oehry

Another gust forced my jacket open and pushed my hood off in the split second it took to snap the picture. I quickly huddled on the ground, back to the wind, blowing warm breath over the skin of my face that had been exposed to the elements. It would take only seconds for the skin to turn into a white frostbitten mass if I was not careful. Crouched low, I fixed my clothing while I was waiting for the slightest break in the assault. The moment it happened, I half-crawled and half-ran as fast as I could to huddle again close to the ground, back to the wind, just a few yards down the trail. It was as though the tempest had taken a deep breath only to return with a vengeance. While it had pushed me from behind on my way up, I now had to face it, fighting my way with every step down the mountain. This was its territory, and clearly I was the trespasser. Eventually I reached my skis and was welcomed by those little frozen trees, the last sign of vegetation I had left behind. This time they looked warm, gentle, and cozy to me as I rested between them, exhausted but completely sheltered. My eyes returned to the peak, which gleamed innocently in the sun.

NONATTACHMENT

Eager for my well-deserved powder run, I retraced my steps on the narrow path along the ridge. At its other end, the Old Carriage Road opened wide, promising good skiing for more than four miles. I had eagerly anticipated this part of my adventure.

As I reached the end of the ridge, I came across a young couple. They had just returned from the smaller South Peak of Mount Moosilauke, eyelashes still frozen white from their own summit battle. They had carried their Alpine skis and boots strapped to backpacks up the mountain. About twenty yards away, I saw a single ski boot, a ski pole, and tracks in the snow. These told me a story of the struggle that had taken place. The young man's boots were frozen solid, the plastic unwilling to give even a quarter of an inch to allow his foot to slip in. Unfortunately it was not as easy for him to stuff his boots under his shirt as I had done with my batteries. I felt great sympathy for his dilemma—sorry for all the lost turns he must have dreamed about during his long and arduous ascent of the mountain. He was forced to hike out.

Buddhism and other philosophies and cultures teach the principle of nonattachment—nonattachment to people and things but also nonattachment to ideas, beliefs, hopes, even dreams, as life always flows differently than we expect. Ancient cultures speak of our bodies having the potential to live as long as nine hundred years. But in order to do so, we would need to learn how to let go of all the hurts in our lives, the pains, frustrations, losses, and all of our attachments to them. We would need to be able to flow with life and surrender to its unexpected turns with comfort and ease. We would need to become fully aware that we are eternally connected with all there is and that losses can only be experienced externally. They never disturb our true inner peace or rob us of our inner wealth. Then we would become peace itself. They say this learning alone would take about seventy to a hundred years—a span that we consider long enough for a life well lived in our present time. I wondered how the young man was fairing and if he was able to let go of his powder dreams and frustrations, surrendering to circumstance.

As I prepared for my own powder dream, my cautious self advised me to leave the skins attached to my skis. The base was thin and plenty of rocks were hidden underneath an inviting layer of powder snow. With my skins left on my skis, I would travel downhill more slowly and consequently more safely. My adventurous self, on the other hand, assured me I was capable of dodging any obstacle and would have great fun playing in the powder for miles to come. In a flash the skins came off. Soon I was turning with ease, powder snow flying high into my face while heaven descended upon me.

Less than half a mile into my heavenly snow dance, I was floating with delight in perfect unison with my body, my equipment, and the terrain. Suddenly my foot turned right, but my ski traveled left. I went "heinie over teakettle." Bouncing down the trail like a Ping-Pong ball, I concluded I had *prereleased*, meaning my binding had opened without apparent reason. Then I remembered I didn't *have* releasable bindings.

I picked myself up, shook off the snow, and gathered the equipment, which was strewn all over. To my dismay, I discovered my binding cable had broken. There was no way to fix the problem with what I had in my pack. I was forced to hike out, forced to give up my own powder dream for the next four miles.

While I gathered my stuff and strapped the skis onto my pack, I remembered the young man, who was probably still at the top of the trail. I smiled because I knew I was the one who was now practicing very hard how to surrender to life's surprises. I smiled because I knew only too well that with my equipment broken, I would be protected from the temptation of skiing past the safe snow cover and onto dangerous rocky terrain farther down the trail. I continued to smile as I hiked slowly down the mountain, because I noticed many beautiful details in my surroundings that I otherwise would not have seen had I been swiftly turning in powder la-la land. Still strongly attached to the dream of turning gracefully in powder, I smiled at the regret that would surface persistently and my struggles with nonattachment as I adored and plowed my way through the untouched powder at my feet.

When I finally arrived at my car, I looked back at beautiful and glorious Mount Moosilauke, shimmering white in the sunlight. This mountain had offered me a bigger bite than I could chew. I was humbled by the forces of nature and grateful for the lessons in compassion and nonattachment. I was awed anew by the infinite beauty of bitter-cold winter days. And I was definitely ready for a long rest in the company of my woodstove, a good book, and a cup of tea.

Astral Travels To Night Universities

Luckily it has not been necessary to gain every insight on this yearlong journey through physically exhausting and challenging experiences. I did not always have to climb a mountain in below-zero temperatures and near-hurricane-strength winds to gain a bit of wisdom. Occasionally I was granted insight in the form of a gift during the hours of sleep. These were planted like seeds into my subconscious mind while I was tucked under a cozy down blanket, sleeping by the comforting crackle of the woodstove.

So it had happened ten months ago when I awoke with the taste of a journey full of learning still lingering in my sleepy mind. I knew I had experienced something important. I had dreamed, but it was more than a dream. I immediately knew I had not actually been dreaming but rather exploring again some other place while I had been sleeping. Such an experience is known as astral travel. As I always did before I went to sleep, I had asked my spiritual guides to allow me to astral travel to places where I could learn and explore while my physical body and conscious mind were asleep. These nightly excursions are different from the garbled dreams that seem to create abstracts from unrelated bits and pieces of our daily lives. During astral travel the physical body stays exactly where it went to sleep, while the spiritual body goes on a journey. At all times the bodies are connected through a silver cord so as to make sure that our physical self will not lose its spiritual counterpart. Astral travel happens quite frequently, but most of the time we do not remember it consciously. The experience stays solely in our subconscious mind. However, when we do remember an astral journey, we know instantly that we have been astral traveling and are usually blessed with great insight and learning from the experience. It is like attending a *night university*. I have made it a habit over the years to jot down those memories linked to astral travel immediately after I wake. The places I have traveled to and the insights I have gained through these nightly outings are invaluable to me.

During my sleep I had traveled to a place in another dimension where other people existed as well. These people, I clearly remembered, were very different from us. They were glowing in a beautiful white light. They did not seem to possess physical bodies, not as we know them, but rather they seemed to be made of pure light in human shape. I immediately noticed that they existed in perfect harmony with one another, strikingly different from what I was used to among my fellow humans. These light beings did not need to speak their words, but instead they were able to express themselves through their thoughts. I knew about telepathy, but these people could see *all* thoughts at *all* times. Minds were visible and open for everyone to read and to understand. This made me keenly aware of and a little uneasy about my own thoughts, which were suddenly so exposed. I noticed the absence of any negative, sad, or sick-minded thoughts. I quickly concluded that they must exist without negativity, sadness, or mental illness, all of which are so prevalent in the societies on our earth. I dwelled in the lightness of these beings and within their peaceful and harmonious energy. Everything within them and around them radiated with light and love. It was a breathtaking experience. It stayed with me after I woke, and I was in awe. I knew immediately I had been granted one of those exceptional gifts of remembrance. I had traveled again, and I remembered each detail well.

Memories of astral travel are not intellectual memories alone. They are experienced and felt throughout the entire body, and the learning becomes an instant knowing. After this astral journey, I knew—not just from research but also from my own experience—that there really was a place where beings lived in absolute love and harmony with one another. There are many fascinating stories about these mystical places. They are called by various names in different cultures. But reading about Shambhala, for example, had never actually convinced me of its reality and its existence. So I was tremendously grateful that I had been given a chance to visit such a place and see for myself.

But I also felt a little troubled by the experience. I did not remember seeing an actual world around these light beings. They seemed to exist in a glow of light. I did not remember seeing trees, plants, flowers, sunsets, or even animals. As much as I appreciated and admired these beings, their harmonious existence, and their radiance of love and peace, I missed our lush earth, the richness of nature, the scent of flowers, the mooing of cows, even the smell of manure. I missed the sounds and the ability to touch and taste. I knew I had journeyed to a place where beings were much more evolved than us. I was shown a way of existence that would be a possibility for humans one day. I understood that we create our reality through our thoughts and that the absence of negative thoughts, sad thoughts, or sick thoughts would make it impossible to have suffering or pain, crime or betrayal, distrust, or even fear. Thoughts of love cannot simultaneously exist with thoughts of fear. What an amazing way to live! What an incredible possibility! Yet I love our earth, and the prospect of not being surrounded by its lush beauty would be hard to bear. Being the honest creature that I am, I thanked the spirit helpers who had guided me to this place. I thanked them for trusting in me, for their love, and for the incredible teachings. But I also sheepishly confessed that I would rather stay here on our earth instead.

It was now a full ten long months since I had had this insightful experience with the light beings. As I awoke early on this crisp winter morning, I instantly knew that I had been given the sequel to my previous experience, or more precisely, a response to my sheepish confession ten months ago. I had been out there again, frolicking in other dimensions, while my physical body was having a nap.

This time I remembered clearly walking along a path, and suddenly with one step, I found myself in another dimension. It was as though I had crossed a pathway or a bridge or traveled through a gate. I stopped immediately in my tracks. One foot was in the old dimension, while the other foot was in the new. The world in the old dimension behind me was the world I was used to living in, a beautiful world of rich nature and diverse people. The world in the new dimension was also like the old world with the same earth, plants, trees, and people, but here everything was brilliant and aglow. I looked behind and then ahead of me several times, lingering on the threshold of this gateway until I decided to step fully into the other side. Here in the new dimension, I found the same light beings I had encountered in my first visit. But this time there were also trees and plants. The entire earth was there, and it emanated a beautiful glow. The people were of that exquisite, light-filled, harmonious nature I remembered so well from my first encounter. I felt a rush of joy the moment I crossed the gateway. Moreover, I was immediately rejuvenated the instant I took a step into this other dimension. My body was glowing like the bodies of the light beings around me, and I marveled at the transformation in myself. I felt so healthy and balanced. I remember thinking how wonderful and light I felt and how good it was not to have any physical ailments. Up to this point, I had not been aware that I even had any physical ailments. But this new state of being let me feel a distinct difference. What an amazing change in me and all around me. I also was very aware of the absence of any kind of need. All necessities seemed to be taken care of. It was more an unspoken understanding than a witnessing of the absence of industry, money, obligations, disease, or suffering. In this place I experienced a blissful existence.

I immediately understood the lesson in this sequel. First I was shown that nature did exist among these beautiful beings, even more magnificently than I could have imagined. And secondly I understood that this brilliant and harmonious dimension was not somewhere in outer space but right within our existence, one step of *awareness* away from where we are now. It could be reached not necessarily by traveling but rather by a state of being. This beautiful and peaceful dimension was the creation of intent, the outer manifestation of thoughts and feelings of those who are aware. It was another plane overlaying our present world, a layer of love and light. It was real, and it existed!

I had glimpsed a new reality, and I could not help but long to return. My internal focus narrowed, and a renewed sense of urgency surfaced. I was already keenly aware of a spiritual support that I knew was present in my life. Now, however, I pleaded to be guided more quickly toward this higher form of existence. I had witnessed those who already have achieved this state, and I could see what lay ahead for us. I also knew that we would all eventually reach this state. It is our destiny.

Ice Curtains

It was now close to the end of bitter-cold February. For many people winter may seem an endless torture, but for ice climbers winter and its different facets comes and goes all too quickly. Ice climbing is generally safe for a little more than two months in New England. Depending on the start of cold temperatures and the altitude at which the ice forms, there may be good climbing during November and December, and there is some climbing in March, which is usually the end of the ice-climbing season. The safest time to climb, however, is January and February, when the ice is typically thick and solid.

We were nearing the end of the climbing season, and I had already climbed many beautiful ice curtains and shoveled what seemed like a never-ending onslaught of snow. The days were starting to get longer, and the sun, which was a little bit stronger now, began to represent a serious threat to the solidity and safety of the ice. I did not want to risk having the beautifully formed ice melt away while my nose was stuck in a book. So when the phone rang and I heard that it was Alexander, my partner in crime when it came to vertical play on ice or rock, I was ready.

Alexander and I often ice-climb at Smuggler's Notch near Stowe, Vermont. Smuggler's Notch is well known for its interesting climbs, and it is also a place surrounded with tales of robbery and other wrongdoing as its name suggests. Though I consider myself a person of reasonably sound mind, I have come to know that ogres live there, waiting to play their mischievous games with climbers. I encounter them every single time I venture into the Notch. They show up in various forms, hiding behind cracks, boulders, and ice curtains. They snicker when they send avalanches down on ice climbers. They steal and eat our ice-climbing gear or throw ice daggers at us. Once, I thought I had them beat for sure, as everything had been going suspiciously well that day. Then they showed up in the form and shape of an ignorant but very fit solo climber who had the audacity to jump on my climb ahead of me. He sent huge chunks of ice flying my way, which consequently had me frozen in place for the next two hours.

Only a couple of weeks ago while we were hanging halfway up an ice climb at Smuggler's Notch, we had done it again. Alexander and I had looked across the other side of the Notch in awe and then taken a picture of our dream climb— Ragnarock! Ragnarock is a long, hard, and suspiciously rocky ice climb with a bulging ice curtain looming at the top. It is considered a mixed climb, which means it will have ice in certain areas and sections of pure rock as well. An ice climber is equipped with ice axes in both hands. Attached to the climbing boots are crampons, metal points that allow a climber to get secure footing on vertical ice. Rock climbing with this gear can be a real challenge. To climb Ragnarock, one had to be able to climb rock with ice gear on hands and feet. It was one of those climbs reserved for the lucky few who could dance up rock or ice with mysterious ease. Wisely we did not consider ourselves part of this tribe. But one of these days—or maybe years—we promised ourselves, when we were suddenly blessed with an unexplainable gift of climbing talent, we would tackle it.

Alexander had heard rumors during the beginning of the ice-climbing season that Ragnarock had "come in" early this winter, meaning that it had formed some climbable ice. Totally ignoring the fact that the calendar informed us that it was already the first of March (and thus nearing the end of ice-climbing season), Alexander had convinced me that we should have at least a look at the object of our desire. We set out early the next day.

The temperatures were supposed to be somewhere in the pleasant thirties, according to the weatherman. When we arrived at the parking lot at Smuggler's Notch, the wind was roaring with snowflakes flying sideways, temperatures only in the frigid teens, a blind fog moving in and out, proving that the ogres were already in full swing and at the height of their game.

After a long hike from the parking lot, following the snow-covered road into the Notch, Alexander and I reached the approach gully leading to the start of Ragnarock. The steep gully was covered with a couple of feet of fresh snow. This meant another forty-five minutes of strenuous post-holing (breaking trail in fresh snow) to reach the base of the cliff. Out of nowhere, three strong Frenchmen appeared and took the lead, leaving deep footprints, making our approach significantly easier. They were heading for a climb near Ragnarock. The Frenchmen apologized for not moving faster, blaming the wine they had enjoyed the night before for their slow pace. Amused, I thought life was looking up, ogres nowhere in sight. As we hiked laboriously upward, we saw an ice climb called "Origin of Intelligence in Children." It looked interesting, and the ice was perfectly well formed. Alexander and I may give the impression of being mature adults, but in truth there is plenty of children's intelligence in us. We thought this climb might make a good alternative to our adventure if things looked dreary over at Ragnarock. We parted ways with the Frenchmen and headed along the tree line in the direction of our climb.

I got there first and took one look at Ragnarock. Immediately I turned and headed back into the shelter of the trees to take care of a sudden urge that had overcome me at the sight of this impressive climb. When you are a girl and you climb, theoretically you have only one chance at this business, and that's at the bottom of the cliff. Once you are in the harness, loaded up with gear, and up on rock or ice, you may as well forget it. So amidst howling wind and flying snow, down came all the layers.

Meanwhile, Alexander arrived and stepped out of the trees to inspect the object of our long-lasting admiration.

He concluded that it did not look "in," meaning that there was not enough ice on the lower pitches to safely climb the route. I emerged from my frigid powder room and readily agreed. Alexander thought we should be realistic and climb something else. Somewhat relieved, I quickly declared his decision a smart choice. Put at ease by our mutual consent, Alexander suggested we should at least try to climb the first pitch, which would be the distance of one rope's length. We knew that at the end of the first pitch, we would find fixed anchors, permanent equipment drilled into the exposed rock, to allow for a safe rappel back to the ground. Of course, I found this to be a fantastic idea.

Alexander carefully worked his way up the cliff. At times I could see him. At other times he was completely covered in spindrift (clouds of wind-blown snow). During some winters nature forms a line of ice all the way to the start of this climb. When that happens, one can climb on ice to reach the enormous curtain of the third pitch without having to bother with rock. Mostly, though, the first pitch has little ice, leading to a difficult second pitch with much exposed rock from which one can finally reach the large breathtaking ice curtain of the third pitch.

I followed swiftly to the belay, where Alexander had secured himself to the fixed anchors. The second pitch was not "in" as we had expected. There was no ice at all to allow for an ice pick placement, let alone placement of an ice screw for protection. Usually the leader hand-drills the ice screw into solid ice and weaves the rope through a karabiner attached to the screw. This is done strategically at precise intervals so that the leader, in case of a fall, is protected from landing on the ground or hitting a ledge on the cliff. However, with no ice present on the second pitch, an ice screw placement was out of the question.

Despite of the unfavorable condition of the route, we studied the second pitch—a steep line of unfriendly black rock. We had brought a few pieces of rock gear in case we felt inspired to go on. In the absence of ice, we could use the rock gear for protection. Scanning the rock carefully, I thought I saw a way to climb it. Alexander suggested that it was my turn to lead. I protested, pointing out that I had no experience leading on mixed ice. With his usual sense of humor, Alexander reminded me that there was in fact no ice on this pitch. And with nothing but rock to climb, he argued, amongst the two of us, I was the better rock climber. I countered that I was equipped with funny things like ice picks in my hands and crampons on my feet, which were not at all suitable for rock climbing. I did not trust myself placing ice axes on rock and safely climbing with crampons in the absence of ice. If I was to be in the lead, there needed to be fat ice ahead. He agreed to give the second pitch a try.

I turned into the most skilled coach you could ever imagine. From my belay I spied tiny cracks for the ice axes and saw placements for the metal points of the crampons, even some possibilities in the rock for protective gear, and I communicated all of this to Alexander in my sweetest voice. It worked. Alexander masterfully climbed the challenging pitch, even skipping a scraggly bush. Had I been climbing in the lead, I would have grabbed the bush with my teeth and strangled it with slings in an attempt to establish protection. It wouldn't have held a mouse's fart.

I followed quickly, marveling at Alexander's courage and excellent climbing skills while placing my ice picks and crampons carefully into small cracks in the rock. I removed the few pieces of protection Alexander had placed and eventually reached him at the second belay. From here the ice curtain looked incredibly tall, steep, and menacing. We studied it carefully and chose a line that would lead us about forty feet horizontally into space before it turned straight up the enormous curtain. Alexander suggested again that it was my turn to lead. He had just led two very technical pitches and was looking forward to relaxing a little. It was common for us to switch leads—that is, unless one of us was not up to the task. He pointed in the direction of the ice curtain looming a thousand feet over the Notch, indicating where I should be climbing. I responded with hysterical laughter.

Longtime climbing partners spend endless hours in cars, on approaches, and tied together on ropes in good or sometimes very precarious situations. You know pretty much every detail about the other person, often more than you really want to know. Alexander knew when to argue and when to let it go. In response to my uncontrolled laughter, his eyes lit up, and there was a hint of a smile around his mouth. This enormous ice curtain was his kind of stuff. There would be solid ice to sink his axes into. He went.

He began the long traverse, placing an ice screw with a karabiner and a long sling about halfway out for my protection. After forty feet of horizontal traversing, he headed straight up the enormous ice curtain and disappeared from sight. He climbed strong, though he was blinded by frosted glasses. Alexander has poor eyesight and depends heavily on his glasses. Often, while climbing, they are either fogged up or iced over. Once, completely fogged up, he even took them off while climbing an extremely difficult pitch, one that I would have had little chance of leading myself. I had known he was just about blind without the glasses, and as I watched him climb that day, I was torn between admiration and utter terror. Today, iced over and fogged up, he looked confident and solid.

I watched the steady and rhythmic flow of the outgoing ropes. It occurred to me he would probably be out of earshot by now. My eyes followed the outline of the steep and rocky cliff below the ice curtain. There were no anchors out there, no shelves to rest on. Should I for some unforeseen reason lose my grip and let go of my ice tools on this forty-foot traverse, I would swing out like a pendulum and dangle below the ice curtain high above the ground. My tools, stuck in the ice, would be out of reach. I did not have them tethered to my harness or body to make sure they would fly with me if I fell. I usually carry an ascender for such situations, though I always hope I will never have to use it. The ascender is a little gadget that allows the climber to ascend a rope should he fall and dangle in space. But the ogres had not been sleeping. I had dropped my ascender at the beginning of pitch two. This mishap occurred, of course, to the ogres' amusement and wind-howling laughter. Now I felt thoroughly naked despite the many layers of clothing I wore.

Alexander out in space on the third pitch of Ragnarock
Photo: Isa Oehry

Hanging from my precarious perch, attached by nothing but slings to the cliff, I decided to put my worries aside for now. Instead I marveled at the extraordinary beauty of my location. High up on this cliff, surrounded by majestic ice, I felt free the way I imagined a bird would feel. With Alexander out of sight, there was no other person around, nobody to watch, nobody to talk to.

WATER, ICE, AND DNA

Every now and then, the snow and fog cleared, and I was allowed a glimpse into the Notch far below—a scenery of a wide range of gray scales. However, by paying closer attention, I could detect a glimmer in the ice. There was indeed a hint of color. Once, while I was climbing on an ice curtain at sunset, I suddenly found myself in a glittering crystal palace. The ice all around had transformed into a deep pink, reflecting the sunset. Today there was no sun to deliver such a spectacle, but among the gray scales, there were slight color variations in the ice, hinting at hidden potential and sudden surprises. Ice is beautiful and mysterious. It is a substance that has many faces. Warm it up, and its particles will become thousands of times more active, making the ice turn to liquid. In its frozen state, its molecules and atoms align with lots of space in between, allowing it to float. That meant that the thousands of tons of ice I was about to climb were lighter than water.

Water is heaviest at thirty-nine degrees Fahrenheit (four degrees Celsius). It's a marvelous trick of nature. As the top of a lake begins to freeze and becomes lighter, the heavier water at the bottom stays a constant thirty-nine degrees. This temperature allows many water creatures to survive harsh winters, comfortably snuggled in the mud below.

Hanging onto an icy cliff and not moving much, I was busy keeping my own bodily liquids from freezing. The adult human body consists of 70 percent water. We actually start out being 90 percent water at birth. We then gradually dry up to approximately 70 percent during adulthood and roughly 50 percent in old age. This means we consist primarily of water. Again I closely inspected the ice around me. It occurred to me that I was mostly made of the same substance just in a different state. (Despite the harsh temperatures, I was not yet frozen.) Alexander, I was certain, would be quite warm, strenuously working his way up the vertical ice and carefully placing protection.

As I looked closer at the ice around me, I detected individual snow crystals, no two alike. These reminded me of Dr. Masaru Emoto's marvelous work. Emoto succeeded in taking pictures of water at the exact instant it changed from liquid to frozen state and formed ice crystals. Through his work he came to understand that water indeed has its own language. When the water was polluted, for example, it refused to form ice crystals. Instead it froze into an unsightly blob. Clean and natural springwater, on the other hand, consistently formed beautiful ice crystals. In *The Hidden Messages in Water*, Emoto published the results of hundreds of empirical experiments involving water.

When Emoto took polluted water that was unable to form a crystal and exposed it to thoughts of healing in the form of meditation, the water transformed and was able to form beautiful crystals. Emoto went as far as to simply tape written words on jars of water and discovered that the water inside the jars responded predictably to the meaning of the words. Water in jars with the written word *love* would create beautiful crystals, whereas water in jars with the written word *hate* would not be able to form a crystal at all. Water proved to be able to detect what we would consider slightest variations in tone, intent, sound, and emotions with incredible accuracy.

What does that mean to us humans as such watery beings? How are we affected by our thoughts and intentions considering the amount of water in our bodies? We already know that memories affect our DNA, but water that had been held by a healer proved to have a healing effect on damaged DNA as well. Since we have thousands of miles of DNA in our bodies and consist mostly of water, could it be that alternative healing phenomena and spontaneous remission are caused by thoughts and intentions absorbed by our bodily fluids, which then heal our DNA?

How were my thoughts and feelings affecting my environment, the ice I was currently looking at, or more importantly, my climbing partner, who after all was presumably at least 70 percent water? Could my thoughts reach and affect the fluids in Alexander's body and change his DNA? He had disappeared somewhere above the huge ice curtain into a gray "neverland." A slight and rhythmic triple pull on the ropes, a signal that Alexander and I share to communicate when out of sight and earshot, indicated he had arrived at the top of the climb and was securely fastened to an anchor. All my attention returned to our climbing adventure, and I focused exclusively on the task ahead.

Once the ropes were tight, it was my turn to follow. With all senses sharpened, I tiptoed and danced out the traverse to the first ice screw Alexander had placed. Here, I swung my ice ax hard to make sure it was lodged firmly in the ice. With one hand I held on to that ice ax. With the other hand, I took the sling, which had served as the directional, and looped it through the opening in the handle of my other ice ax. I clipped the sling to my body with a karabiner. Now, one of my two ice axes was fastened to my body. I potentially could only lose one. If I fell, the other would travel with me. I knew that with at least one ice ax, I would be able to maneuver my way up almost anything. Now my mind was at ease, and I was focused on nothing else but the great and steep ice ahead.

I worked hard, swinging the axes with great force, trying to achieve secure placements and firmly kicking my crampons into the vertical ice. Ideally as much body weight as possible should be on the small metal points of the crampons. This technique keeps weight off the arms. On steep curtains like the one I was climbing, good technique is crucial. Yet my forearms soon began to ache, a sign that I was pulling too hard on my arms and not following good technique. A quick look up the curtain showed me how far I had to climb until I reached a small stance, a bulge in the ice that would allow my foot to stand flat so I could give my arms a quick rest. In this way I managed to climb the enormous curtain, accompanied by much groaning and moaning, and I eventually reached Alexander. It was almost dark. He greeted me with a big congratulatory hug. Today, though, he deserved all the hugs. He had led this challenging climb in great style.

We attached headlamps to our helmets and prepared for rappelling. Rappelling is always exciting. Rappelling over the edge of an ice curtain into a black void is especially exciting. With the help of the headlamps, we were able to find the rappel anchors as we carefully lowered down the ropes. After three rappels we arrived safely on the ground. We quickly packed our gear, coiled the ropes, and slid down the approach gully, hooting and hollering like little kids. Tired but exhilarated because we had climbed and survived Ragnarock, we began the long hike back to the car. (The hike was now at least three times longer than on the way in—another mischievous trick of the ogres.) Once we arrived at the parking lot and sorted out the climbing gear, we noticed that an ice screw was missing, a treasure to a poor climber and a favorite morsel of ... well, you know who.

Ragnarock was the perfect adventure to end the ice-climbing season. I was ready to say good-bye to Mr. Winter. In my pursuit of pranic wisdom, the ice had generously shared much mystery hidden within its molecules. Now it was beginning to melt. I happily stored away the ice-climbing gear in anticipation of warmer temperatures and began dreaming of spring.

Part IV

Spring

Spring Traditions And Hazards

In spring, the sun gains a more direct angle in relation to Vermont's latitude, and we actually begin to experience some warmth. Everything starts to melt at an astounding rate. Finally (and greatly appreciated) spring arrives.

But before the meadows turn green with surprising suddenness, we suffer through a season I have encountered only in Vermont—the notorious mud season. Of our roughly fourteen thousand miles of roads, an impressive eight thousand of them remain unpaved. And Vermonters like it that way. During winter the dirt roads freeze solid, sometimes to a depth of four feet and more. When temperatures finally start to rise, the roads begin their thawing process and transform into merciless car traps. Cars sometimes get stuck up to the doors in mud only to be rescued by a friendly neighbor and his tractor.

Mud season in Vermont
Photo: Nick Goldsmith

There was once a photograph on the front page of the *Rutland Herald* that showed a disgruntled driver staring at his car in disbelief. The car was stuck up to its roof in mud, and he had apparently escaped through a window just in time. A crane in the photo was trying to pull the car from the bottomless trap. Readers so sympathized with this fellow that the majority never noticed that the picture was published on April Fools' Day.

Eventually the longer hours of sunshine prevail and manage to dry the roads. In the woods small patches of dirt appear, and the very first and long-awaited plants begin to sprout. Then, seemingly overnight, everything turns green. But spring has more surprises in store than mere vegetation. The warmer temperatures not only lure cabin dwellers out of hibernation but also welcome critters of all sizes and shapes.

Contrary to what you might expect, it is not the biggest creatures that are noteworthy but the tiniest, the *Ceratopogonidae*. This spelling challenge is commonly known as the "no-see-um," because these insects are so small you can't see them. Despite their miniature size, they bite viciously and make you itch like there is no tomorrow. No-see-ums show up at sunset, but they have an even worse competitor that does not care about the time of day and likes to hunt you all day long. It is its cousin, the black fly, a particularly skilled hunter. It sneaks up on you, numbs your skin with a little venom, takes a malicious bite, and proceeds to suck your blood. Having satisfied its hunger, this rascal leaves you with blood still dripping from the bite. There are 1,800 known species of black flies, of which eleven are now extinct. In my opinion, extinction seems the most appropriate fate for this nuisance. I have declared war on them, and I am planning on outliving all 1,789 remaining species!

Officially spring starts with the vernal equinox around March 20. Despite this official date, a critter that many gardeners consider a vexation seems to also have a say in this matter. The *Marmota monax* are energetic troublemakers and persistent about their mission. Commonly known as groundhogs or woodchucks, they can weigh up to twelve pounds. They favor homegrown vegetables over any other greens and can clean out a garden bed and erase the hard and proud work of weeks within an afternoon. They pop out of the ground in unexpected places, establishing a convenient den entrance within your garden or nearby. Not only are they a bother to gardeners, but farmers dread them as well, as cows and horses can break a leg stepping in one of their den entrances. Even tractors have been known to overturn by catching a wheel in a burrow.

On February 2 each year, millions of people in the United States expectantly await the emergence of this cute rascal from his den. It is believed that if Mr. Groundhog sees his shadow on that day, he will quickly retreat to his burrow, and winter will last another six weeks. This brings us conveniently near the twentieth of March. On the other hand, if Mr. Groundhog does not see his shadow because the weather happens to be all but sunny, it is said that winter will have a quick ending and that spring will come early. Traditionally this little digger has been in charge of announcing the end of the winter since 1841, when the German tradition became known through a diary notation of a storekeeper in Pennsylvania.

In Vermont, groundhogs are smart and enjoy a much longer snooze. Their hibernation lasts well into April. It is Town Meeting Day, the first Tuesday in March, which marks the unofficial beginning of spring regardless of what the weather is doing. Town Meeting Day is a tradition still held dear in Vermont, and it dates back to 1762. On Town Meeting Day, residents all over the state gather in town halls and school gymnasiums to elect town officials, vote on local budgets, and debate the pertinent issues of their community. These days meetings are often quiet and scarcely attended. Sometimes, however, they are anything but boring. Disgruntled by the politics of the federal government, the residents of Brattleboro and Marlboro voted in 2008 to arrest the US president and vice president, sending a message beyond the borders of their towns and Vermont, drawing national attention.

Wisdom Of Plants

On Town Meeting Day, Vermont is still often covered in snow. But for many it is the long-awaited day when the first tomato seeds are planted in growing pots and placed by windowsills. With increased daylight and the warmth of the woodstove, these seeds will develop into little seedlings. Come May, they have grown into hardy starter plants and can be transplanted into the garden.

Vermont has one of the shortest growing seasons in the United States. Since record keeping began, frost has been recorded over the years in every month, even in July. Creativity is required when it comes to gardening in Vermont. But after a long and cold winter and a landscape that offers nothing but whites and grays for months, many Vermonters can't wait to dig their hands into the dark and scent-rich soil to begin the process of growing their own food.

Unable to garden for many months of the year, I have come to appreciate my houseplants in a special way. I have a grapefruit tree in my bedroom that my daughter planted from seed when she was a toddler. The tree has grown over the years to reach the height of the ceiling. I have become very fond of it and have developed an unusual kinship with it. It is the first thing I see in the morning when I open my eyes, and it is not entirely out of the ordinary for me to speak to it. My cat once brought a bird into the house and—only accidentally, I am certain—let it get away. I tried to rescue the poor animal but remained unsuccessful as it fluttered from room to room. It finally crawled under my bed as daylight diminished, and then it became quiet. I quickly shut the door, opened the window, and removed the screen. I figured the bird would find its way out come daybreak. Sure enough, at the first sign of dawn, I noticed movements under my bed. I remained absolutely still. I expected the bird to fly straight out the window. Instead, however, it flew up into the grapefruit tree and sat on a branch, facing the open window. Here it lingered. I wondered why it did not embrace its freedom immediately. As I observed, I became aware of the plant. There was a sense of excitement coming from the tree itself. I realized that for the first and possibly only time in its existence, it was graced with the presence of a real bird. In its natural environment, the tree would be interacting with insects and birds daily. But here in my bedroom, this visitor was an extraordinary exception. Finally the bird fluttered out the window and was gone. I continued to look at my tree, wondering what this experience had meant to it.

Before you declare me completely insane—conversing with plants and claiming to sense their emotional state—let me introduce you to the field of plant communication. The research began with Cleve Backster. In his day Backster was a leading expert in the field of lie detectors. He ran his own school, where he trained police and security experts from all over the world how to use these devices. One night he had a strange idea that would change his life forever. He attached a lie detector to a plant that was growing in his office. He was curious and wanted to find out if the plant was capable of any reaction that he could detect. While he was looking for an appropriate way to experiment with the plant, the idea of burning one of its leaves crossed his mind. To his amazement, at the very moment of this malicious thought, the needle of the lie detector jumped. Puzzled, he left the room to fetch some matches, and when he entered his office with matches in hand, the needle jumped again. Apparently, he concluded, the plant could read his thoughts and intentions. After this night in 1966, Backster's life would never be the same. He gave up his work as a trainer for lie detectors and dedicated the rest of his career to exploring the secret life of plants. During his extensive research, he discovered that plants not only had the ability to read thoughts and intentions but could also recognize people.

In one such experiment, Backster directed six students to pick a note from a basket. Only one note carried the instruction to destroy a plant in the laboratory. For the experiment each person was to walk through the lab alone. Neither the students nor Backster himself knew who the actual plant killer would be. The plants in the lab were going to be the only witnesses to the killing.

The students passed through the lab one at a time, one student destroying a plant. Backster then attached a witnessing plant to a lie detector. All of the students were now directed to walk through the lab again one at a time. Five times the lie detector was quiet, but when the actual plant killer passed through the lab, the needle went crazy. The plant remembered the killer and could distinguish the plant killer from the other students.

Backster was curious about whether plants could go as far as telling the difference between the truth and a lie. He designed a simple experiment involving a journalist. He attached a plant to a lie detector to find out if the plant would know if the journalist was lying about his birth year. Backster read out loud several years, including the year the journalist was born. Prior to the experiment, Backster had instructed the journalist to answer with no to every year, including the year of his birth. When the actual birth year was read and the journalist answered incorrectly, the needle on the lie detector jumped. After the journalist published these as yet unbelievable results, many labs reproduced the experiments and confirmed them.

Backster then tested his plants' responses over a distance of several miles. He enclosed the plants in Faraday cages, cages that do not allow radio frequencies or other signals to penetrate them, to make sure no electromagnetic signals were being transmitted. But in all cases, the plants responded to Backster's thoughts at exactly the same moment he produced them. Still suspicious that he may have influenced the plants himself by his thoughts and feelings, he constructed an experiment where human thoughts and emotions were eliminated altogether. He built a small mechanical device that pushed living crabs into boiling water at random intervals. The crabs were killed instantly. The device was placed in a room *adjacent* to his lab and plants. It automatically and precisely recorded its own movements. He then attached a plant in his lab to a lie detector and left the building for the night. He could not know when the device killed the crabs. The next morning he discovered that the plant with the lie detector attached had responded at exactly the same time the crabs were being killed. It appeared that the plant could sense the crabs' trauma through the walls of the building.

Backster's crab experiments finally earned him recognition by the scientific community. His study was published and widely recognized at the time. Later, however, his work was brutally debunked by skeptics, causing the research on plant communication to ground to a halt for the better part of two decades.

After Backster's work had been disproved, plant communication researchers were looked upon with ridicule. Skeptics cynically suggested that these researchers were wasting their time studying something that had already been debunked. Today, after much thorough research and carefully controlled experiments in labs and in the field, plant communication has staged a powerful comeback. According to Richard Karban, an ecologist at the University of California and AAAF (elected fellow of the American Association for the Advancement of Science), the debate is no longer whether plants can sense messages, but how they do it. It is now well established that plants communicate with each other. Under attack, they release volatile organic compounds. These compounds signal alarm to other plants. In response to the warning, the plants quickly join the conversation and in turn release their own chemical cocktail containing powerful messages. Well informed about the upcoming danger, they take action, and make their leaves less tasty to damaging and hungry bugs, encouraging the bugs to go elsewhere. Or, they choose to release distress signals that will attract other bugs, which are capable of fighting the intruders.

Recently, Ted Farmer of the University of Lausanne discovered, that plants also communicate by means of electrical pulses. A plant's elaborate root system suggests another means of communication. We don't know how many roots a single tree has, say Peter Tompkings and Christopher Bird in their book *The Secret Life of Plants*. But the research on a single rye stalk has yielded a sum of more than thirteen million small roots, which would reach a length of 380 miles if laid out in one long line. In addition, each root has very fine hairs growing from it, approximately fourteen billion per rye stalk. If these were connected into one long row, it would reach 6,600 miles, according to Tompkings and Bird. In comparison, the distance from the North Pole to the South Pole, if measured through the earth, reaches 7,900 miles.

Three decades after the beginning of his research, Backster was again recognized for his groundbreaking work. He was awarded multiple honorary doctorates and other awards by prestigious establishments. Even though, we still do not understand the actual way Backster's plants were able to read his mind, remember people, know truth from a lie, or sympathize with dying crabs, it is now well understood that plants do indeed chat with each other, respond to external stimuli, and are able to send, receive, and decode messages.

Since plants do not have eyes to convey their emotions or the legs or wings to express themselves visibly, it is hard to imagine that they have a spirit. However, something within plants is obviously keenly aware and in touch with their surroundings.

I was sure that my grapefruit tree was not ignorant to the fact that a couple of delicate bird feet had gripped one of its branches. And with present day plant communication research, I could be certain—even without a lie detector—that it was chatting excitedly about its visitor. I suspected that it was also aware of my personal thoughts and feelings. I noticed nothing unusual immediately following the bird's visit and continued to feed the tree with the same tap water I always used. Soon after this incident, however, it sprouted a new branch. Not only did it grow a branch of significant size in record time, but the leaves on this branch grew visibly larger than any others it had produced in its twenty-year-long existence.

Rock Spirit

I had not been idle since the arrival of spring. The garden was tilled and fertilized, and the first frost-resistant seeds were already in the ground. With the ice melted, I had replaced my ice axes and crampons with rock shoes and a chalk bag. To my delight, the sun had dried the cliffs, making rock climbing possible even while there were still remnants of ice and snow in shady cracks and corners.

I enjoy rock climbing for a variety of reasons. I love touching, feeling, and even smelling the rock. When the sun heats up the stone, it becomes comfortably warm and begins to give off the faintest of smells—the pleasant scent of rock. Working my way up a climb feels like yoga in a vertical world. While I am climbing, I am twisting my body gently in every possible and impossible posture just to reach a fingerhold spied somewhere above me.

I pursued climbing since my early twenties while I was growing up in the Swiss Alps. Even back then as a novice climber, I remember respecting the spirit of the mountain. Often while I was camping at the foot of a major climb, I would get up at night and speak quietly to the mountain, asking it to be gentle with us the next day and to keep my climbing partner and me safe.

It was early April and a beautiful spring day when I found myself sitting on a dry spot at the bottom of one of Vermont's climbing crags. I was leaning lazily against the warm rock, instinctively becoming aware of its spirit. It was not as though it was chattering into my ear, and I wasn't getting internal messages. No, it was the gentlest presence of something alive within the rock that I was feeling. I know for sure that animals have spirits, and I know that plants also have spirits. But I have always known that rock has a spirit as well, deeply entombed, moving at an infinitely slow rate, and it was aware of my presence as I climbed all over it.

From my comfortable spot at the foot of the crag, I could study the impressive line that Alexander, my climbing partner, had discovered last fall. The line—the section on the cliff we hoped to climb—wove its way over three small overhangs and led to a large massive overhang. Underneath this enormous overhang loomed a rock flake spanning the entire width. At the beginning of the overhang, one had to climb upside down, using the flake for good handholds, and then continue, applying the same climbing style all the way to its end. Then one had to turn around the edge of the overhang and finish the climb on the vertical cliff above. For people who aren't climbers, imagine your kitchen ceiling as the overhang with a crack reaching from the kitchen door across the ceiling to the window. This would be the flake. You climb up the kitchen door, reach the crack, and then proceed upside down like a fly along the crack to reach the open window. You climb through the window, grab the exterior siding of the house and continue up along the outside until you reach the chimney. Of course, a real cliff has many tiny holds and cracks that allow climbers to get good grips for such insensible and pointless undertakings.

Attempting the difficult move to turn the corner
at the edge of the overhang
Photo: Isa Oehry

Establishing a rock climb in Vermont involves hard work. Our cliffs are often covered with lichen and are seldom of solid rock quality. Alexander and I had established countless new lines over the years, enjoying the challenge of opening up climbing routes for our own pleasure and for others to follow. To begin a new route, we typically start cleaning the rock along the suggested line, scrubbing it with wire brushes and tossing anything loose to the ground. Trundling rock was not my specialty. I never liked the sound of a falling rock, either tossed intentionally or flying off the cliff by its own volition. So I gladly give Alexander credit for the majority of the preparation for our climbs. It had been the same with this new line. He had pointed it out to me the previous fall while we were climbing another route nearby. At the time I took one look at his suggested line and declared him insane. Unimpressed by my reaction, he began the cleaning process immediately on his own, roping in from the top, cleaning the lichen, and trundling loose rocks. His efforts were eventually interrupted by the arrival of winter. But as soon as the ice melted, he was at it again.

Now six months later, I was relaxing at the base of the same crag underneath Alexander's project. Alexander was busy drilling permanent bolt anchors along the new line. All the preparation work was finished, and the exciting task of establishing the climb was well underway. It was my job to feed Alexander rope while he slowly progressed upward. This was often a time-consuming task. It was hard work for the person doing the drilling and easy work for the belayer, and it could take hours. I did not mind, as the time I spent belaying my climbing partner was never lost time for me. My eyes watched his every move, while my body automatically performed the necessary belaying functions. This gave me the mental freedom to reminisce.

I was intrigued about our adventure. The prospect and excitement of climbing upside down like a fly made me forget my initial apprehension about Alexander's suggestion to develop the line. Yet when he had picked me up in the early morning, I had again felt hesitation. Sitting at the bottom of the cliff and basking in the pleasant spring sun, I began to gently stroke the rock with my free hand. I asked its spirit to be good to us and to keep us safe.

When Alexander was done drilling, I lowered him down to the ground. It was now my turn to give this crazy climb a try. I was excited about monkeying out the horizontal flake underneath the large overhang and learning the moves. Alexander had drilled two permanent anchors alongside the flake. These anchors would be crucial to my safety. I would clip my rope to them with a karabiner and a quick draw (a short sling) to keep me off the ground just in case I took a fall.

I quickly climbed past the three small overhangs to reach the large one. Tucked underneath it, I had a good look at the horizontal flake. It was impressive and made me instinctively cling to the vertical rock behind me. Yet the flake promised good hand and toe placements all the way to the outer edge of the overhang. How I would turn the outside corner, I was not sure. A bit apprehensive yet excited, I took a deep breath and committed. I reached out as far as possible with my arm and firmly gripped the flake. Then I swung a leg up and stuck my toe behind the flake. I was upside down, hanging like a monkey. This was fun. Horizontal and upside down, I proceeded slowly to the end of the flake. There I hoped to reach around the corner and find a good hold on the upper vertical cliff. It was the most technical and difficult move of the climb. I tentatively groped for a hold with one hand. To my delight, I found a small crack in the rock, one big enough to offer a solid grip. With both my legs jammed into the flake, I was hoping to pull myself up and around the corner with my arms while I pushed with my legs. I knew this was a one-time shot. Either I would succeed, or I would have to return to the ground to start over. I gave it my all along with some impressive bilingual sound effects, pulled and pushed, and then pulled and pushed some more. But the smaller overhangs below were causing friction to the rope. The rope was not gliding freely and allowing me to move upwards. Suddenly my feet lost their grip and slipped, and my fingers, not strong enough to hold my weight without the help of my feet, let go. I fell into space.

The rope and Alexander's anchors caught me a hundred feet off the ground and about twelve feet out from the vertical cliff, dangling in midair. Laughing, I asked Alexander to lower me down to the ground. We had had enough excitement for one day, and we decided to come back in a week and give the climb another try.

Dangling in midair after an unsuccessful attempt
Photo: Isa Oehry

The following week we ventured out again. I had used the intervening time to work out the moves in my mind, and I knew I had a good chance of succeeding. Yet I felt the same hesitation the morning Alexander picked me up. It was unusual for me to feel this way when we were heading to a small crag versus a big mountain climb. I shrugged it off and looked forward to the excitement of trying to surmount the tricky overhang. This time Alexander was going to lead up to just under the large overhang, anchor himself, and then belay me up. From there I would lead out the flake, experiencing little rope drag, and hopefully my chances of succeeding would be better.

While Alexander was busy climbing, I again found myself speaking to the spirit of the rock. I knew that the spirit within rock was not necessarily less evolved than a human. Elisabeth Haich, the author of *Initiation*, states that a spirit often experiences various forms of existence. Through its evolutionary journey, it moves first through the mineral world and then the plant and animal worlds, and finally it exists as a human being. Once human, its life cycles revolve around inner growth and soul evolution with the ultimate goal of again returning to its initial pure state of divine consciousness. At this state a spirit is able to understand and manipulate energies and universal laws at will, says Haich. But it comes with responsibilities. It is in fact a razor-sharp path with lurking dangers around each and every corner because the temptation to channel higher energies into the physical self for one's *own* benefit (to acquire such things as money, status, and power over others, for instance) will cause an already evolved spirit to fall far below the human state. Could such a fallen spirit find itself in the next life embodied as an insect or maybe even as my nemesis, the black fly, or worse, entombed in a rock for thousands of years with no ability of expression at all? I wondered if the spirit I felt in this cliff had once reached the highest state of consciousness in human form but had floundered. If so, imprisoned in rock, it would be millions of times wiser than I was at the present moment.

I heard Alexander's voice announcing that he was safely anchored. I put my thoughts about the rock spirit aside and quickly climbed up to his belay under the overhang. From there with the comfort and support of my climbing partner close by, I used all my focus on the task at hand and proceeded out the horizontal flake, again upside down. At the end of the flake, I applied the moves I had visualized over the past week. I reached up high with one arm, gripped the small crack in the rock, and pushed with my legs, twisting my body in such a way that it could upright itself. With much huffing, puffing, and vocal expressions, I slowly made progress inch by inch until I finally stood upright with nothing but my toes resting on the tip of the flake. I had succeeded in turning the corner without falling or grabbing any draws I had clipped to the bolts. Exhilarated, and without much rope drag, I quickly climbed the twenty yards of vertical cliff above to the anchors. Here I securely attached myself and hollered a joyful yodel at the top of my lungs into the valley below me. Then I began belaying Alexander.

Since Alexander was underneath the overhang, I could not see him from where I was anchored. I needed to be careful not to pull too hard on the rope, otherwise he would lose his balance. I couldn't pull too little either. That would give him poor protection. As if the rope was an umbilical cord between us, I gently felt his moves as he climbed upside down along the flake. Once he reached the end of the flake, the movements stopped. This was his first try at the difficult edge. I knew he was looking around, trying to figure out where the fingerholds were. Suddenly I heard him holler for a tight belay. I gripped the rope and pulled it hard, securing it with the belay device. Then a sudden tug on the rope followed as he took a fall. Luckily he was close enough to the overhang that he was able to grab the quick draws I had clipped to the bolts and lift himself up and over the edge. Laughing, he climbed to where I was anchored. We rappelled, packed up the gear, and decided to go out to dinner, which was a rare treat for us, to celebrate our success.

Only two days later, we were back. I again felt the now familiar uneasiness when we approached the cliff in the morning. Alexander had used the short time to ponder the difficult moves, and he was eager to try the climb without taking a fall. This time I swiftly led to the anchors under the overhang and belayed him up. We changed leads, and he proceeded upside down in gecko style along the flake toward the edge of the overhang. Moving slowly and deliberately with much physical effort, Alexander succeeded with the difficult moves. He turned the edge without falling or grabbing any slings and skillfully managed to put his body in an upright position. From my belaying spot underneath the overhang, I could only see the heels of his climbing shoes extending out from the cliff. Here he stayed for a while. I leaned far out on my rope, trying to see what he was doing; however, the overhang was too big, and I was directly below. He let me know that he was busy calming his nerves and gathering his wits from the pure thrill and exhaustion of the difficult moves. Eventually he continued and climbed the vertical cliff above to the anchors. Already familiar with the climb, I followed quickly and reached a happy Alexander. We rappelled to the ground and sat on a comfortable rock directly underneath the climb. Here we rejoiced and celebrated while we gathered our equipment.

On the hike back to the car, my mind returned to the spirit in the rock. I thanked it anew for keeping us safe this day. I also wondered if, by recognizing and acknowledging its existence and by giving it a chance to grant us the not-so-small favor of keeping us safe, it would in some way be redeemed from its miserable existence and allowed to return to its former human state. I kept these thoughts to myself as usual.

A couple of days later, Alexander called, clearly shaken about something. He had returned to the crag together with a friend with the intent of showing him the new line, our most exposed and exciting climbing route yet. But when he approached the cliff, he found that the entire large overhang of our climb, including several bolts he had placed, had fallen to the ground. The massive rockfall had crushed mature trees and destroyed our comfortable sitting rock immediately underneath. The bolts, which had caught my first fall and from which I had dangled in midair while I was laughing about my predicament, were also gone.

Alexander stopped at my house on his way home to show me the pictures he had taken of the disaster. As I looked at images of the enormous hole in the cliff and thousands of pounds of rock scattered over the ground, I knew for sure that we had been protected from this imminent disaster the entire time we were there. I knew that my feelings of apprehension had not been a mere fabrication of my imagination and that my gentle requests for protection had been heard. This was confirmed when Alexander shared with me that after he had turned the overhang on his successful attempt and was standing at its edge, gathering his wits, he had felt the slightest of eerie movements under his feet. I had been anchored directly underneath the overhang, underneath thousands of pounds of rock that were beginning to fall but somehow did not.

From my past experience I knew that the spirit, if it were truly present and responsible for protecting our lives, would leave a symbolic message. I began zooming in on the pictures, scanning the huge scar in the rock for anything unusual. And sure enough, in the middle of the gigantic hole that the rock fall had created in the cliff, there was a perfectly shaped heart about a foot in diameter!

The gigantic rock fall and the heart
Photo: Isa Oehry

Any time one lives through a close call, one enjoys a renewed sense of aliveness. This latest experience made me appreciate my life with an even deeper awareness and a sense of urgency. It was not that I was afraid of dying. No, I had glimpsed other dimensions, and from those experiences I knew that we had ultimately only a blissful existence to look forward to. But I understood that each life in human form is a precious gift, offering ever-present opportunities for growth. The possibilities for growth I had glimpsed during the course of this year alone seemed infinite. I felt as though my mind and my awareness were expanding. I was eager to discover more. I knew very well that I had merely scratched the surface of something profound.

Furthermore, it would have been terribly irresponsible for me to leave my remains behind, scattered over the ground to be delivered to my daughter in a shoe box. Certainly this scenario would have been worse than an arrow stuck through my throat, and packaged into a shoe box, there would be no way to explain myself. So I was more than glad and thankful that our lives had been protected. This was definitely an occasion that called for celebration. Alexander and I went out to dinner, this time to celebrate nothing less and nothing better than being alive!

PART V

SUMMER

LAKES AND PONDS

I enjoy the few hot and humid days of summer with every ounce of my being. These days are numbered and can be gone before you realize that they have arrived. In Vermont, you are never quite sure if you are experiencing a long and late spring lasting into June or an early fall starting in July. At some point between these two seasons, a few days of precious hot and muggy summer weather occurs.

Savoring each summer day, I do what many Vermonters do. I spend much of my free time by the water. The ponds, lakes, and rivers of Vermont are treasures for wildlife. Nothing delights my heart more than the soft yodel of a loon through the early morning mist or the slap of a tail on water announcing my intrusion into beaver territory. One time I saw a mama bear lead her young to the water for a drink. Another time I observed an enormous moose dip its head underwater in search of the grasses it favors.

With a few days of hot summer weather, Vermont's lakes and ponds warm to inviting temperatures and lure folks— even those like me who think they have more in common with mountain goats than with fish—into their smooth and silken waters. Swimming the circumference of a small lake is a thrill to me each and every year. The Alps, where I grew up, are a relatively young mountain range formed *only* sixty-five million years ago. Its lakes are deep and bitter cold. These bodies of water are seldom enjoyed for casual swims. Rather they lend themselves to quick dips of lightning speed, accompanied by bloodcurdling screams. Fed by glacial ice water all year, they never have a chance to warm to pleasant swimming temperatures. Vermont, on the other hand, is situated along Old Appalachia, a mountain range stretching from Canada southward all the way to the Blue Ridge Mountains of Georgia. These

Appalachian Mountains are among the oldest in the world. They were formed some 1.1 billion years ago when the earth's crustal plates collided. The earth behaved rather hellishly and expelled extreme heat and pressure starting some 450 million years ago. Fairly recently over this vast expanse of time—only three millions to twelve thousand years ago—glaciers covered the earth's surface. Through their eternally slow yet ceaseless, pulsating motion, they smoothed and sculpted the jagged mountains to form the gentle hills of the Green Mountains of Vermont. This glacial activity also shaped the many wonderful shallow lakes and ponds that I have come to appreciate so much.

CREATION AND RESOLUTION OF KARMA

It was now July and pleasantly hot and humid. Summer definitely had arrived. In pursuit of cooler temperatures, I had loaded my canoe and put in at the Hartford Dam, a little known state park in Vermont. With no other access or development, this is an area particularly rich in wildlife. Because of the enormous dam, the water is calm, and though it is a river, it behaves much like a lake for a stretch of four miles. My eyes automatically scanned the shore for movement as I slowly paddled, following an internal rhythm while contemplating my journey. I never in my wildest dreams during that full-moon night last fall could have imagined a journey as mysterious and life-changing. What started with a spontaneous decision to find out what I could about prana and its legendary wisdom had quickly transformed into a much bigger adventure. If you were to see me lazily gliding through the water in my canoe, outwardly you could not tell anything special was happening, yet inwardly I was experiencing a revolution.

I had paddled roughly one mile when I spotted a bald eagle perched in a tree, its white head and tail clear indicators of its maturity. From its size I guessed that it was a female. They are usually larger than males. It looked peaceful and calm, but I knew better. Underneath its sleepy appearance, it would be keenly aware of any movement in its surroundings and in the water, ready to lift off and dive at an astounding thirty-five miles per hour to catch its prey. I decided to linger nearby and wait.

My thoughts returned to my journey. By now I understood that the universal substance of which our thoughts and feelings are made is obedient to our conscious will. It responds *unconditionally*.

I remembered the fable of the man who was remorseful for spreading untruths about someone in his village. The man visited an old sage and asked how he could possibly repair the damage he had done. The sage advised him to go out immediately and place a feather on each doorstep of his village and return the next day. The man did as he was told and returned the following day to await further instruction. This time the old sage told him to go collect the feathers and bring them all back. Bewildered, the man said that surely in the meantime the breeze had carried them away in all directions. And so, answered the sage, it was with the untruths he had spread.

The instant our thoughts, feelings, and words are released, they rush out into the universe like the feathers blown away by the wind. If destructive in nature, they create disharmony, and the universe demands that harmony be reinstated. The universe does not tolerate disharmony. It will provide opportunities over and over again to remedy the situation until balance is restored. This can be a most lonely and often painful journey, as nobody can take the place of the one who created the manifestation. Here we must face every crisis alone. It is the creation and resolution of karma.

My eyes remained fixed on the eagle. I could see that its head was pointed in my direction. The eagle is on the top of the food chain. It has no enemies. I was not a threat to its livelihood. Nor was I in the way of its hunting. We continued to remain motionless. My thoughts returned to the creation and resolution of karma. I was relieved that there was a means to remedy all the chaos and turmoil I had created, intentionally or not, in this lifetime or even in previous lives. I was also beginning to understand that when negative thoughts are sent out at random, even if not directed at a specific person, these thoughts are drawn to like-minded others—people we may not know—like a magnet. By letting loose an avalanche of random negativity, we create karmic connections with these strangers. The disharmonious connections will require resolution at some point. This, I came to understand, is the reason we experience so many small but annoying circumstances in our lives involving complete strangers.

In our culture of surplus and affluence, we have little understanding of these facts. We freely let our emotions play out their drama and allow our brains to think whatever comes to mind without any understanding of responsibility for thoughts or feelings. There is a moment, however, just when the discordant thoughts or emotions (e.g., anger, hate, worry, or fear) have entered our mind, that we are still able to wrest control. In that split second, we have a conscious choice. If the negative energies are permitted to rage unabated, that moment of control is lost. The discordant thought or emotion is created and sent on its way only to return to us later, heavily laden with its own kind. Not even an atom will escape along its journey. Thoughts and feelings are real, living, pulsating things. In essence, there is no need to be a hero in this world. There's no need to defend a kingdom, save a damsel in distress, make a fortune, or become famous. Just to be able to *abstain* from contributing to negativity on a daily basis—in controlling one's thoughts and feelings—would be true heroism.

In theory, it seems easy. But I knew that if I wanted to journey further, I needed to be stronger than I had ever been before. I saw the path ahead. It was steep and quite narrow. On either side were pitfalls, a yin-yang existence symbolizing emotional ups and downs. Should I slip to one side of the path, I would find pain, fear, despair, hate, and depression. To the other side, I would find the sweet earthly pleasures, intense but fleeting joys, likes and dislikes, attachments, and strong yet uncontrolled emotions. If I managed to stay on the narrow, razor-sharp path in the middle, only then would I find lasting bliss, peace, and real unconditional love. I sensed that eventually this path, which required so much control and willpower now, would widen and become a natural and effortless way of being. To get there, however, I was certain that I would stumble many more times. I would have to pick myself up repeatedly, dust off my knees, and carry on.

Suddenly the eagle lifted off its branch and swooped down. It flew an elegant half circle and then barely touched the water's surface. Its flight uninterrupted, the eagle rose from the water with a foot-long fish in its talons. Still much alive, the fish wiggled in a futile effort to escape its deadly fate. The eagle returned to the tree, perched, and began consuming its catch.

It all happened in seconds and left me in awe. The eagle is a bird of enormous size with a wingspan easily extending beyond seven feet. Being able to observe it in flight within yards of my canoe made it appear even larger. I saw its piercing eyes clearly, intently focused on its prey as it swooped by me. I noticed the impressive yellow beak, curved down with a sharp hook at its end, and its deadly talons.

The eagle's beak and talons are its weapons. It used these now to tear the fish into pieces. It swallowed some and tossed to the ground the parts it disliked. It was a vigorous act the eagle performed with absolute certainty and purpose. Transfixed, I watched and realized that we need equal certainty and purpose if we desire to control our thoughts and feelings.

Unity And Oneness

Thrilled, I paddled back to the Hartford Dam, where I had set in, and returned home. Nature never ceases to teach me—usually in most unexpected ways. During July and early August, I took many more trips to local lakes and ponds, observing, learning, and simply enjoying myself. Soon, however, I had to pack a warm jacket on these trips, as days became shorter and temperatures dropped abruptly after sunset. Glorious summer was already nearing its end.

It was the end of August when Tim, my sweet and fun friend (who back in January would rather have warmed his tootsies under my covers than climb Mount Moosilauke), invited me to his house for dinner. Our times together were special, and we both cherished them. Delighted, I quickly packed ingredients for home-baked bread and set out to meet him.

After a joyous hug at his doorstep, we gathered vegetables from his garden and began preparing a meal. There was electricity and anticipation in the air the moment I arrived. I could smell the scent of his skin as he walked from one corner of the kitchen to the other, busily arranging and sorting vegetables of every color and size. While I was mixing the dough, I reached up and gently brushed against his strong neck with my lips. It was just a tease, a quick *hello* from my body to his, a message that told him how excited I was to be sharing time with him. Close to my ear, he let me know how strong his feelings of love and desire were for me. His breath was warm against my skin as he whispered. Quickly I stood on tiptoes, reaching for his lips. I could feel the heat of his body as we kissed. We continued to prepare the meal, aware that the night was ours. Time and the rest of the world had ceased to exist. We had moved to our imaginary island where there were no other people, no phones, no duties, and no obligations.

This night was about us, about returning to this place of indescribable oneness, a place of bliss and happiness we vaguely remembered from some long-ago time in a faraway place.

Once the sweet smell of freshly baked bread escaped the oven and the delicious scent of herbs and spices filled the air, Tim lit the candle and placed a bottle of homemade wine on the table. The food was ready. We took our seats and filled each other's plates with delicious steaming vegetables and slices of freshly baked bread. We marveled at the colors and textures, remembering the origin of each ingredient. While we were refilling glasses and plates, our hands gently touched now and then. We laughed and talked; our conversations were never boring or superficial. We took our sweet time savoring the meal and each other's company.

The last drops of wine gone and hunger satisfied, we stacked the dishes in the sink. I was just beginning to wash them when Tim gently turned me around and surprised me with a long and passionate kiss. I responded willingly by letting my lips part. His mouth was soft yet eager and warm, and he tasted sweet and pleasant. My hands moved along the familiar outline of his arms and chest. I unbuttoned his shirt and felt the warmth of his skin. The familiarity surprised and delighted me anew, causing my body to respond with deep longing. He brushed the shirt off my shoulders, kissed my bare skin, and skillfully undid the clasp of my bra. Shirt and bra fell to the floor as his lips continued to explore. A sweet smile crossed my face. No longer would the kitchen accommodate our playing. Slowly, our eyes locked in mutual desire, we reached for the candle and began wandering upstairs to the bedroom, touching, kissing, and teasing with every step.

The bed was soft, and the old quilts felt warm against our skin. There was no longer a need for words. Our lips were having the conversation. At times they touched. At times they barely brushed the skin, taking in each other's breath, caressing face, neck, body. I delighted in rediscovering his eyes, tracing the line of his straight nose with my lips, and returning to his warm and eager mouth. I closed my eyes and enjoyed the sensation of his touch. Then I opened them again to see his familiar face in the candlelight. His eyes were closed, on his face the slightest hint of a smile filled with pleasure. The air was rich with unstoppable desire. Our bodies were longing for unity. We slipped out of the remaining clothes.

I reached up to him, drew him closer to me, and felt his strong and muscular body against mine. He lingered, taming his eagerness in appreciation of the imminent bliss to come. I savored this moment before the moment, dwelling in the anticipation of being even closer to him, united and one. I tried to hold myself back but could last only what seemed like a fleeting moment. Overcome with desire, I offered my deep well of pleasure to him. Aware and experienced, he took his time to accept the offer fully, sending sparks through my body and causing my mind to lose its grip on reality. A moan escaped my lips and mingled with his sighs. Nothing in life seemed to compare to the depth of these feelings. Our bodies, hearts, and souls were melting, becoming one, returning to a faraway place where we had never been apart. In that moment we both understood the eternal meaning of love. We had found what every being on this earth is looking for. We had found unity, oneness. We continued to move in harmony as though we were trying to find a place even more united—until we could hold back no longer.

His arms wrapped tightly around my body, we rested, illuminated by the light of the candle. He gently kissed my face and whispered sweetness into my ear as I drifted into a peaceful sleep. I woke again to watch him sleep, a gentle smile still lingering on his face. Our arms were intertwined as if we wanted to make sure we would not lose each other ... ever. A bird called outside the window. It woke him, and we listened to it. He knew what kind of bird it was and why it called in the dark. Still in each other's arms, we fell asleep again.

Bits of light managed to work their way through the curtains, announcing a new day. It was still early, and we chose to linger, hoping that each minute would take two to pass. It had been a night so pure and sweet, a night I could only wish for everyone who tastes the sweetness of love for the first time. It was a night worthy of a Shakespearean pen.

We listened to the melody sung by the first morning bird, joined quickly by an entire choir. Time and the world were returning. Reluctantly we rose, washed, and dressed, still savoring each moment together, wishing there was no world outside our little orb. We were both uplifted by our togetherness, the sharing of our love for each other. We tenderly kissed as we parted.

I drove away, dwelling on sweet memories of our togetherness. Hours after our lovemaking, my heart still hummed with the melody of each word spoken and each moment shared. I could feel him lingering with and around me, and I treasured the feeling.

However, quietly and ever-so-slowly, a familiar but persistent longing made its way back into my awareness. Separated from Tim, the fleeting nature of sexual bliss, even if shared with great love and tenderness, was ever so apparent. The feeling of deep oneness I had experienced during our union seemed but temporary. Something inside me yearned for an infinite union with heart and soul— eternal oneness.

I sensed that it was impossible to become truly one with another, even if committed through deep love and marriage. We can make a decision by using our minds and hearts to unite our lives and walk our paths side by side, to share experiences and support each other along the way. In such a union, we may experience beautiful moments of oneness; however, the instant we are separated from the other, there is an unmistakable gap that brings back the reality of our incompleteness.

Slowly I felt Tim's energy retreating from me. I sensed him wandering into new corners and crevices, as if I had a little window into his world through which I was, intentionally or not, peeking and taking part in his life. Somehow I had remained connected to him in more than just an emotional way. While Tim and I had been intimate, our energies had intricately and deeply intertwined. We had exchanged our love, spilled out the innermost feelings of our hearts, and shared our bodies. Such an intense exchange creates much more than an emotional connection.

WANDERLUST OF CELLS

The U.S. Army Intelligence and Security Command (INSCOM) conducted an experiment that demonstrated how people stay connected to an astounding degree, even after days of separation. During the experiment researchers scraped cells (from the roof of the mouth of a poor fellow willing to hold open long enough) and placed them into a test tube. The fellow was then separated from the test tube and hooked up to a polygraph that recorded even the slightest physiological changes. The cells, alive and well in the test tube, were hooked up to a polygraph as well. The subject was asked to watch movies that would stimulate various emotions ranging from soothing and calming to disturbing and exciting. These emotions (joy, pleasure, sadness, anger, hate, fear, or repulsion) would cause physiological responses. The researchers kept a keen eye on the subject as well as the test tube, and they discovered to their surprise that though physically removed, the cells in the test tube registered the exact same physiological response—at the exact same instant— that the subject produced in response to the movie. The researchers continued to separate the individual from the test tube farther and farther apart. At a distance in excess of fifty miles, two days after the cells had been scraped from the subject's mouth, the cells still registered the same activity at the exact same instant.

Contrary to our twenty-first-century doctrine, there is no such thing as casual sex, as every interaction is an energetic physiological entanglement. Two people engaged in sexual intimacy not only share their love, tenderness, and passion but also exchange an innumerable number of cells. While lovers engaged in a monogamous relationship exchange cells exclusively with each other, a promiscuous person entwines energies and exchanges cells with many.

This individual carries a medley of cells from one person to the next, depositing some and picking up others. According to the experiments done by INSCOM, any cells left behind by Tim would be responding to his new adventures at the same time these adventures were taking place. It was no surprise that after the romantic night with this passionate man and our deep sharing of love—and also, no doubt, our extensive cellular exchange—I was very much aware of exactly when Tim began to withdraw and direct his attention to another. He was happily mixing the cells I had deposited with him, all of which were still very much connected to me, with new cellular companions. The various emotions born through his new adventures were becoming part of my cellular vocabulary. Involuntarily I was not only part of Tim's emotional life but also entangled emotionally and physiologically with his former, present, and future lovers.

Positive And Negative Poles

My desire to reexperience oneness and unity was strong enough, that I repeatedly chose to disregard what I knew about our unruly cells. The longing for this exquisite bliss can cause all else in life to fade into the background. I was not alone, however. Throughout history this longing has prompted kings and queens to renounce their royal positions and leave kingdoms and riches to follow the call of love. The feeling of blissful unity and oneness has caused husbands to leave their families and wives to leave their marriages. There are stories in which love has given superhuman strength to seemingly weak people. At times people have committed insane crimes for the same reason. Our history, legends, and tales speak of countless examples, telling of people who have longed for and set out to find this bliss, bliss so deep and all-encompassing, it overrides all sense of logic and reason.

Elisabeth Haich, who wrote extensively about this topic, states that this longing is born out of our human nature, because we carry the knowledge and memory of oneness and bliss within the deepest core of our being. It lingers within us like a faint, persistent memory, and we look for it all the time, whether we are consciously aware or completely unaware of it.

Haich teaches that every being contains within itself a positive and negative pole, a male and female pole. Absolute peace, stillness, and balance are only present within the divine state, where positive and negative poles are united. In the divine state of absolute stillness and peace, no creation exists. All simply is. For creation to take place, poles need separation. Separated from its opposite, they will constantly and without interruption seek to reunite again, causing tension and pull between them. This tension and pull is the underlying force that drives evolution.

Each creation does contain both poles, Haich further explains. But because we identify with our physical bodies, we are unaware that we carry both poles within—positive and negative, male and female. Hence, we tend to express ourselves as only one pole, either male or female. Therefore, our physical selves, which are looking for unity and completion, are constantly seeking the opposite poles. Not knowing that both poles are actually *within* us, we seek the missing poles *outside* ourselves, hoping to reunite. Through sexual union we experience moments of this blissful state of oneness and completeness.

A Secret Deeply Buried Within

Within this beautiful act of creation, there is also buried a deep secret. It is the secret to life itself, says Haich. It contains the key to our existence, the blueprint for our life's path.

Within each human is embedded the desire to grow and to evolve into a better being. Sometimes this desire is buried deeply under the surface, but it is still present. At times it seems completely gone, covered by pain, hardship, and suffering, or hidden by the self-seeking desire for power, status, greed, and materialistic things. However, it is always present, and many miraculous changes in people have proven its existence. This desire is the pull of our two poles, says Haich, each seeking reunion with its opposite. It strives for the ultimate goal of reaching highest consciousness. And it is the sexual power itself that houses the secret of how to reach this goal.

Many have reached this goal successfully. Many who have come to the end of their journey have returned to help the rest of us struggling to find our way here on earth. From all over the world and from various cultures throughout history, we have recognized those who have returned as masters and teachers. Through their teachings on all continents and in different cultures and languages, we have learned about this secret hidden within us.

Once one has comprehended this secret, life and its many moments of restlessness and turbulence are understood. Life can be lived consciously, purposefully, and joyously. This secret constantly and incessantly demands that we remember it. Its knowledge is within each of us, but it's deeply buried. It will unfold as an infinitely slow evolutionary process that can span eons if we remain unaware of it. Discovered, however, its process can propel us forward into full awareness, sometimes at what seems lightning speed.

Haich warns, however, that this process demands a natural unfolding. No step can or should be skipped. Just as an elementary school student has to climb the ladder through high school and undergraduate studies to reach and understand the graduate-level teachings, we in life have to walk the path of experience, compiling knowledge on top of knowledge until we finally reach the place of wisdom. Just as the elementary school student would feel confused, overwhelmed, and frustrated if placed into an advanced master's degree program, we would feel the same way if we tried to skip steps in this process. The process is meant to be experienced without emotional or physical suppression. Only in this way will it serve us along our journey.

Underlying this evolutionary process is nothing less than our immense sexual power, states Haich. The sexual power we harbor within is a force that has no comparison. Its singular purpose is creation. Built up, it must seek a release. And if it is inhibited and unable to create new life through a sexual act, it must find another outlet. Unreleased, the sexual pressure will seek a discharge through our higher nerve centers instead, which have their seats in our chakras. The chakras in turn serve as transformers for the unspent sexual energy, setting in motion a process that will ultimately alter our entire being.

In the process of transforming the energy, the chakras change and become charged with a higher frequency—an increased absorption of light energy (prana). The higher frequency then stimulates our intellect and awakens our consciousness. And so it is through the sexual power and its transformation rather than the expelling of it that our higher nervous system is activated and the mind stimulated, awakening and raising our consciousness.

Unaware, we slowly transform over the course of innumerable lifetimes from beings seeking not much more than personal satisfaction while we are still quite animalistic in nature to individuals capable of deeply caring and loving others. As we continue to develop and are able to absorb more light energy and gain more awareness, we begin to seek higher goals in life. Eventually, with our higher nerve centers fully opened, we become aware of our creative power within and are able to glimpse secrets of creation and eternal existence. In light of this higher awareness, sexual bliss gradually moves into the background. We prefer to use our strength and power for our creativity instead. Being able to absorb even more light energy, we eventually are able to develop to a point where we no longer perceive a need to express creativity in physical form. We understand that the highest state of bliss comes from expressing ourselves—not physically—but through a divinely inspired mind, explains Haich. Those who reach this point are no longer the same as the average person. The powers they have gained give them the ability to destroy all harmful viruses and bacteria. They are immune to disease. The unspent sexual power sustains their bodies with strength, vitality, and youthfulness. They no longer experience the desires of the body, the longing for completeness, and the search for the opposite pole. They have become whole within themselves. We know them as our masters and teachers.

All of humanity will eventually reach the highest step of this process. However, this cannot be accomplished without experiencing every step along the path. Life will always draw us back should we attempt to circumvent our desires and longings. The mind will be incessantly occupied with exactly that which we try to avoid. Therefore, Haich emphasizes that desires should not be suppressed. Once enriched and satiated with the experience, we will be naturally ready to move on to the next step.

Road Map

I realized that here in front of my eyes had unfolded a perfect road map of my earthly journey. It was as though someone had snuck up behind me and turned on a floodlight, illuminating the path ahead. I could see myself clearly on this path and the long road ahead to reach the final goal.

I felt immensely intrigued and inspired by Haich's teachings, but at the same time, I was utterly overwhelmed. I instinctively knew of its truth. Once we know something and understand it to its core, it is impossible not to know it. Deeper understandings always shift everything within our perspective until all the details of our newly acquired reality fall into a harmonious order. In the beginning of this journey, I had longed for clarity and wisdom. I wanted to understand how to satisfy my soul's hunger for inner peace and its hunger for a deeper understanding of life. I wanted to be able to use all my energy to learn and grow so that I could become the best expression of myself. Suspecting that it was possible, I wanted to find out how to be free of disease, maybe even aging and dying. And more than anything, I longed for the deep sense of unity I recalled from some other place and some other time. The memory was faint, but it was strong enough, that I remembered being whole and complete, existing in a state of peace. To my astonishment, I had found answers to all these questions by understanding the gift of prana, the role of our chakras, and the immense potential we have by transforming the sexual power we harbor within.

I had learned enough that it would take me a lifetime to ponder and absorb it all. I saw the world as a place in which to learn, grow, and evolve, inching nearer to my ultimate destination. I longed to break loose from the tentacles of thousands of lives lived in oblivion and from their karmic grip on me. I was aware of how easy it is to forget the bigger picture and become distracted by the many diverse and colorful temptations of our daily lives. I realized just how inviting it is to let myself fall deeply into the depth of physical and emotional pleasures, to give up vital energy for sweet and fleeting moments spent in bliss. I came to know that such moments would never satisfy me completely. It also became clear that nothing needed change here on this earth. All was absolutely perfect and had served its purpose and would continue to do so. All was exactly as it should be, even Tim, my man of love and passion.

CALL OF THE MOUNTAIN

Summer had come to an end, and with it, the end of my one-year journey in search of prana and its wisdom was nearing. I had distributed prana to each of my chakras more than 360 times, increasing the amount on a daily basis. I had cleansed, nourished, and energized them without interruption since the beginning of this journey. They became so familiar to me that I could see them with ease, spinning, absorbing, and radiating. I understood their importance and continued to discover new aspects of their purpose.

Throughout the past year, my daily meditations had brought me to a place of deep wonder, appreciation, and gratitude—and to my surprise—at times to a state of bliss that was incomparable with much else in life. Insights had flooded my consciousness during these quiet times. But I also understood that each insight merely opened a window into a new world that was still foreign, waiting to be explored.

There was one more significant adventure that would take place before my one-year journey was completed. Back in March, I had casually spoken with my friend Ernie about our mutual love for rock climbing and mountaineering. Ernie was the straight shooter and dependable travel companion who, back in January, had thought that there would not be enough snow to skin up and ski down Mount Moosilauke. Experienced and cautious as always—he had been right.

In March, our conversation had touched upon the many great peaks we dreamed about ascending one day. As climbers, we tend to develop secret admirations for peaks all around the world. We thrive on other climbers' adventures on these mountains, their successes, difficulties, and failures. We are eager to learn from their experiences.

We want to know every detail of their climbs and weigh our strength and endurance against theirs. In the end, however, most dreams remain nothing but sweet dreams.

But this time, Ernie and I decided on the spot to climb one of these peaks come fall. Organized and always eager to make plans concrete, Ernie had gone ahead and booked our flights for the beginning of September, a full six months in the future. At the time I was unaware that this trip would coincide with the closure of my journey. And of course, as always, I had no clue about its significance and how it would tie all the events of the past year together.

It was the very beginning of September and a beautiful sunny day when Ernie and I stood at the foot of our admired peak, the Grand Teton. I drew in my breath in awe of its magnificence and stature. I had harbored a secret love affair with the Tetons from the moment I first saw a picture of these fantastic mountains, part of Wyoming's Grand Teton National Park. They line up majestically and overlook a high plateau generously populated with elk, reindeer, and buffalo. In the middle of the Teton Range, the Grand stands out like a mighty father, reaching a height of 13,770 feet. To one side, it is flanked by Mount Owen and Mount Teewinot, and to the other side stand the Middle and South Teton, all reaching heights between 12,300 and 12,800 feet.

On our first day in the park, we had climbed Mount Teewinot to acclimatize to the altitude. It had been a long and beautiful nine-hour hike, requiring little technical climbing. There are sections where some climbing parties opt for use of ropes and technical climbing gear. Ernie and I had studied the description of the approach carefully and had decided to free-climb these, because it meant we only had to use light and small daypacks (instead of heavier climbing packs loaded with technical gear). In short, we were able to move faster. This turned out to be a good decision, as we were met at the top by a threatening thunderstorm surprising us from behind the peak. The storm sent us scurrying down the mountain in a hurry, and luckily it did not turn into a torrential downpour until we had arrived at the car. After we climbed Mount Teewinot, we took a day to rest and spent the time preparing for our big ascent.

Our ultimate goal was to climb the Grand. To accomplish this, we had planned one day for the long hike (via the Garnet Canyon Trail) to the Lower Saddle at 11,600 feet, carrying food, water, camping gear, and all our technical climbing equipment. The idea was to establish camp at the Lower Saddle. The next day we planned to ascend the Grand via the legendary Lower and Upper Exum Ridge, an extremely exposed and technical rock climb. This climbing route, which offered plenty of spice and excitement suited to our abilities, is a spectacular climb along the entire sharp edge of the Grand, leading to its summit. We had acquired a bivouac permit from the park service for two nights in case the weather was not cooperative and we needed an extra day to summit. It was a reasonable plan.

It was early morning on the third day, the day we had planned to hike to the Lower Saddle. Ernie and I parked our rental car at the beginning of the Garnet Canyon Trail. This trail is a little more than six miles long and ascends some four thousand feet onto the Lower Saddle, which connects the Grand with the Middle Teton. Rested from our Mount Teewinot climb and well prepared for our big adventure, we were excited to tackle the long approach to the Saddle.

As I stood next to our car, it took me several tries to get the large pack on my back. I was strong, but being strong is always relative. The pack was simply too heavy. I was not used to carrying such a load. At the airport our luggage had weighed in at more than fifty pounds each. So Ernie and I had decided to pay extra for the third bag, which weighed another thirty pounds. Yesterday during our rest day, we had split all the gear as best as we could and stuffed everything into the two huge expedition packs that we now carried on our backs.

View of the Grand flanked by Mount Teewinot on the right
and Middle Teton on the left
Photo: Isa Oehry

I swayed back and forth, trying to find my balance. I could not imagine how I would make the fifty yards to the end of the parking lot, let alone the six-mile and four-thousand-foot ascent to the Lower Saddle. We had started early to allow a full day for the trek with plenty of time for breaks if necessary. I knew Ernie was bigger and physically much stronger than me. I assured him that it would be okay if he hiked at his own pace. Hopefully we would meet up at the Saddle at the end of the day. Sure enough, the last I saw of Ernie was the back of his huge pack as he marched out of the parking lot at a brisk pace. I was on my own.

Slowly and methodically I began the trek. I used hiking poles to take some of the weight off my knees. It helped tremendously. I found a rhythm and began to enjoy the solitude of the early morning. I was only occasionally interrupted and passed by small groups of day hikers carrying light packs. Some of them had attempted the Grand with full gear themselves at one time, and with knowing smiles, they expressed great sympathy for my heavy load. I continued my slow pace, precariously balancing my pack, eyes fixed on the trail. In retrospect, it was a good thing I had no idea how difficult the hike would be. I might not have attempted it at all.

About a mile into the hike, still in relatively low altitude, I again seriously questioned my ability to reach the Saddle with this heavy weight on my back. I was moving too slowly, at times swaying like a drunken sailor, and I was afraid to put the pack down. I suspected, once down on the ground, I might never get it back on. While I was grumbling in my mind about the seemingly impossible challenge of ascending the next four thousand feet, for no apparent reason I lifted my eyes off the trail. Ten feet away to the side of the trail stood a marvelous stag with a rack any whitetail buck would have envied. His gaze was fixed on mine. He was muscular, stoic, calm, and not at all alarmed by my appearance. On his forehead between his eyes, he had a dark marking that resembled an eagle in flight, wings spread wide. From this marking a white stripe of fur ran down to the tip of a shiny black nose. His ears seemed way too big for him, and they had white fuzzy tips at the ends. He kept his dark eyes locked with mine. We stood a long time. While our eyes were intently focused on each other, I felt he was offering me a generous gift, a gift of strength and energy beyond my imagination. I instantly knew I would be able to make the trek to the Saddle.

I continued the hike, amazed at my newfound strength, willing body, and cooperative mind. I silently thanked the stag. Many times I had experienced the surprising and uplifting gifts of the animal kingdom, so I was less amazed than grateful at what had happened. My consciousness, no longer focused on my physical exertion, shifted back to my surroundings. I paid attention. When squirrels bombarded me with pinecones, I ate, and when I heard the soft gurgling of a hidden brook, I drank. My body stayed strong, and my energy remained surprisingly high.

At an altitude of about nine thousand feet, far above any squirrel habitat, I carefully maneuvered my way through a dangerous section of boulders. These boulders, the size of small buses and larger, were stacked the way they had fallen thousands of years ago. Their arrangement left gaping holes, traps that could easily swallow a hiker, pack included. I imagined slipping and falling through a hole, my heavy pack trapping me within a dark never-never land, where nobody would find me for years. But I made it through, bleeding only slightly from scrapes on my knees. I was rewarded with a breathtaking view of the Middle Teton on the other side. I had arrived at the Meadows, a beautiful and lush plateau that was fed by the melting water of the glacier above. I had reached an altitude of 9,300 feet. A feeling of accomplishment came over me, typical for a first-timer on this trail, one who had no clue of what was yet to come.

Following my quickly passing moment of delight were grueling switchbacks. They were incredibly steep, and the footing on the trail was tricky. At the end of the switchbacks, there was a rise that I believed to be the Saddle, my final destination for the day. Encouraged, I pushed on despite my complaining body. Once I had reached the rise, however, I realized that I had merely climbed to the Middle Teton glacier moraine. From here I finally did get a glimpse of the Lower Saddle. It seemed miles away with tiny little dots I recognized as the permanent emergency hut and the shelters belonging to the famous Exum Mountaineering School.

Everything in me protested. But I knew I was much closer to the Saddle than I was to the car, which was parked miles away by the trailhead. There was only one direction for me to go, and it was uphill. So I took heart and continued to put one foot in front of the other slowly and deliberately. The ground was nothing but gray rocks that had fallen from the Grand and Middle Teton over the years, the air filled with a mist produced by the glacier moraines. I stopped looking up from the trail. I didn't want to start expecting the Saddle to be closer than it really was.

After what seemed hours—but in reality was probably no more than one hour or two—I reached the bottom of the Saddle. Here the hiking trail ascended a small cliff maybe eighty feet tall. To protect hikers, ropes had been placed on the cliff and left behind. Normally scrambling up these cliffs would have been child's play for me. But the heavy pack and my state of exhaustion made me gladly and thankfully grab the ropes for extra safety. When I reached the end of the ropes, I had finally arrived at the east side of the Lower Saddle. I spotted a tiny yellow tent neatly tucked behind a huge bolder. It appeared like a brilliant sun in a vast land of grayness. Ernie had already arrived as expected, and he had busied himself putting up our fancy hotel room. Finding our tent already set up was such a wonderful sight. I could have kissed him with gratitude.

Soon after my arrival, Ernie tucked himself into the tent and went to sleep, but despite my exhaustion, I was wide awake and overcome with curiosity. It was still daylight. I decided that I had enough time to get settled in later. Without my pack, which I had dropped next to our tent, I felt superlight. I wanted to see the top of the Saddle, investigate our approach for the next day's climb, and chat with the mountain guides about upcoming weather. And I was excited to possibly see a sunset at 11,600 feet. This would be a real treat for a resident of Vermont. After all, our tallest mountain, Mount Mansfield, reaches only a proud 4,393 feet. I was not disappointed. The view from the Saddle toward the west was spectacular. But instead of a glorious sunset, I saw a black band of clouds covering the entire horizon in the distance. At remarkably short intervals, lightning bolts zapped through the black curtain, shooting in all directions. I innocently asked a guide who had approached the top of the Saddle with me if this was possibly a concern to him and his clients. With years of mountain-guiding experience and a twinkle in his eyes, he assured me that lightning never struck the Saddle. But, he added, if things should go from bad to worse, the guides would, even though it was against policy, allow a climber in despair to find shelter in their permanent and heated hut.

Our "yellow hotel" on the Lower Saddle
Photo: Isa Oehry

Alarmed, I rushed back down to our tent. Totally inconsiderate of Ernie's enviable sleep, I quickly announced my arrival and moved in. Our "hotel room" was small for one person and extremely packed with two bodies and all the gear inside. It threatened to burst at the seams. Within minutes a ferocious wind picked up, a precursor of the massive storm that was to come. As soon as I had zipped shut the entrance to the tent, the sky opened. The storm lasted all night, tugging and tearing at our tent. The sky lit up innumerable times with lightning, and roaring thunder echoed through the mountains. Eventually the downpour was followed by snow and sleet. Nobody slept that night up on the Saddle, not even those guides and their lucky clients in their comfortable hut.

Listening to the merciless attacks of the ferocious wind, I had lots of time to think. Long before Ernie and I had decided, sometime back in the spring, that we wanted to climb the Grand Tetons in Wyoming, I had read much about these extraordinarily beautiful mountains. For hikers, rock climbers, photographers, and nature lovers, these mountains are a dream. I also had learned that there was a lot more going on in these beautiful mountains than hiking and climbing. In fact, much has been written about the Grand Tetons, describing them as a spiritual hub of some sort.

Once upon a time, so the story goes, man was capable of visiting the legendary Shambhala and other sacred enclaves like Shangri-La. It is said that he used to possess knowledge of their locations and took great efforts and pains to reach them, trekking through secret, seemingly impassable pathways and up steep and treacherous mountains. It is said that records of past civilizations and golden ages were stored in these locations and that they served to anchor certain energies on behalf of mankind. When man had turned from his divine path and taken the fall into darkness and oblivion, so the legend goes, these temples and retreats were shifted from the earthly into the etheric plane. Here they would be protected from the ignorant, fearful, and destructive nature of man. Only a few of these retreats are said to have remained in the physical plane. The most advanced students could still reach them, but for the rest of us, they were unattainable. With the birth of the Aquarian Age, however, the honest seeker would again be given the opportunity to enter these retreats and learn the ancient wisdom. The retreats' locations were often described to be in or near mountain ranges, extending deep into the mountains themselves. The mountains, protected through fierce and unpredictable weather high above man's lower vibrations, would keep the unaware and ignorant from reaching them.

I chuckled, lying wide awake in my warm, puffy sleeping bag, enjoying a taste of fierce and unpredictable weather myself. There was nothing like a full-blast storm at 11,600 feet, rain thrashing against the walls of our tent and gusts of wind unsuccessfully trying to catapult us off the Saddle. I had read that deep within the range of the Grand Tetons was the Royal Teton Retreat, one of the few retreats still anchored physically within the earth. The descriptions and accounts of those who had had the privilege of visiting this mystical place had awakened my curiosity so much that I had made this trip to Wyoming, hoping not only to summit the mountains of the Teton Range but to find out for myself if there was any truth to the legendary story.

According to the teachings, a seeker in the Aquarian Age, which would be ours, could travel to these retreats at night during sleep by means of astral travel, leaving the physical body behind. To my astonishment, I had learned that not just hundreds but thousands or even tens of thousands of students attend these universities of the spirit during sleep. In the beginning the conscious memory of these visits would be lost. Subtle changes and insights would, however, occur afterward in the person's daily life. Later these subtle changes would become cornerstones that would lead to a deeper understanding of life and better decision making for the student. Gradually, however, remembrances of these visits would linger. First they would appear like a dream. Later they would take on a clear memory with impeccable detail of the visit, and the teachings would remain.

The Royal Teton Retreat is considered the most important retreat for those who are new at this business of journeying in etheric form while sleeping. Just being near such a retreat is said to give a seeker access to greater energies, a physical and spiritual recharge.

As the hours crept by without sleep on my part, I enjoyed a dynamic recharge of my batteries from the electricity in the air, the rolling of thunder, and the relentless tug of wind on our tent. I never slept a wink. The alarm did not wake us but simply announced that it was 4:30 a.m. and time to roll out of the tent and prepare for our ascent of the Grand.

Traces Of Ancestors

We crawled out of our "hotel room," all bundled up in winter gear, beams from our headlamps lighting the way. A fierce and icy breeze greeted us. The storm of the night had brought winter weather in its wake. A bitter-cold wind forced its way through the Saddle and up along the exposed Exum Ridge of the Grand. Ernie and I changed our plan on the spot. Not willing to fight the icy breeze all day along the exposed ridgeline, we decided to tackle the easier Owen-Spaulding route on the northwest side of the Grand instead.

After a quick breakfast of cooked oats and hot tea, we hiked the long and steady incline of the approach to the Owen-Spaulding route. The steep trail was covered in patches of snow and ice—accumulations from the previous night's storm. Slowly, dawn approached, revealing thick clouds, which restricted any views into the valleys below. The first light of the day also allowed glimpses of the gaping cliffs of the Grand for fleeting moments. But fast moving fog covered them again quickly. Like a skillful magician, the fog changed our surroundings from a mystical land of vertical rock, hovering above an ocean of clouds, into a gray world of mist framed by an invisible yet ever-present abyss.

When we reached the beginning of the belly-crawl traverse of the Owen-Spaulding route, some four hundred feet below the summit of the Grand where technical climbing is unavoidable, we met a climbing team on their retreat from the route. Climbing the Owen-Spaulding route instead of the Exum Ridge turned out to be a rookie decision. Not familiar with the mountain and its weather patterns, Ernie and I had not been aware that the Owen-Spaulding, although technically the easier route, had encountered its first winter assault in late August and had never recovered from it. Crucial climbing sections had remained iced over and would be extremely tricky and possibly dangerous to navigate. The guide of the retreating team advised us to abandon our plans for safety reasons. The route was too iced over. Instead, he offered, we should follow him and his clients to the Enclosure Peak, a lesser-known but worthwhile peak reaching 13,285 feet. We had never heard of this mysterious peak, but technically it was the second highest in the Teton Mountain Range. It was not on any of our maps either, we learned, because it was not differentiated enough from the Grand to warrant its own status as a peak. Yet the short climb to Enclosure Peak was well worth it.

It had also been a worthwhile discovery for the first white man who had summited the peak. Believing he was the very first person to ascend the wild and virgin mountain, he was quite surprised to find an array of elongated rocks, each three to four feet long. The rocks were arranged in a perfect circle like an enormous flower petal. It is believed that the Native Americans once used this incredibly exposed location for their sacred ceremonies. Honoring their tradition, the circle to this day is kept in perfect condition.

Stone circle on Enclosure Peak–13,285 feet
Photo: Isa Oehry

This peak was a thrilling place to linger. Clouds and fog moved in and out, occasionally allowing a glimpse thousands of feet down the sheer vertical sides of the mountain. After the guided group had left, Ernie and I each took a turn sitting in the stone circle, contemplating its original purpose and the bravery of the natives. Many years ago they had ventured to this height without the technical gear of our time—an impressive feat indeed. Eventually we descended back to the Lower Saddle, looking forward to a gourmet mountain meal.

Ernie and I had made a huge mistake, however, when we had planned this trip—putting me in charge of the food supply. This was a grave error, we soon came to realize, because I never paid attention to calories and had no idea how much a strong young man could eat. Generally I am fine with a chunk of cheese and a loaf of bread anytime I venture into the mountains. We had already consumed all our bread, cheese, and dehydrated vegetables. We had drunk our hot cocoa rations, and we didn't have much more than powdered pea soup and some oats left. Nevertheless, dinner at this altitude was simply delicious.

Enjoying dinner at the Saddle
Photo: Isa Oehry

After we washed out our pan and cleaned the utensils, Ernie crawled into the tent and went to sleep. Amused, as it was still daylight, I ventured back up the Saddle in search of a sunset. This time I was not disappointed. The sun presented me with a breathtaking hour-long display. The sky was painted in bands of deep red and orange, surrounding a ball of fire the color of blood. The sunset spread out along the entire unconcealed western horizon before disappearing far below where I stood. Happy and satisfied, I returned to our tent, crawled in, and prepared for well-deserved sleep.

Before Ernie had disappeared into the tent, we had agreed to give the peak of the Grand, which had eluded us by just a few hundred feet, another try the next morning. Sleep, I thought, would be a good start for that endeavor, yet it was not to come. As I lay there, warm, cozy, and ready to doze off, I felt energized and extremely alert. After I had climbed Mount Teewinot a couple of days ago, hauled a huge pack and myself up the grueling trail to the Saddle, and then climbed Enclosure Peak today without any sleep the previous night, I had expected to be pretty close to dead at this point.

I listened to Ernie's regular and peaceful breathing. *Lucky bastard*, I thought. I drifted into daydreaming, experiencing our mountain climbs all over again, and I thought about the mystical retreat that was supposed to be somewhere around here. Was it possible that I was camped right on top of it? It was just remarkable how alert and energized I felt at this point of our adventure. I had exhausted myself beyond belief, had gone without sleep and only eaten a little food, yet I was wide awake, a far cry from being tired. Something definitely was affecting me in this place. While I had been hiking to the Lower Saddle the previous day, my eyes had been drawn to a particular section of the Grand Teton Range. I had wondered if it was possibly the area of a secret entrance mentioned in some of the books I had read.

A couple more hours passed while I mused and entertained myself with my thoughts. Then suddenly I realized Ernie had stopped breathing. I listened closer. His sleeping bag was not moving up and down regularly, and no sound had replaced his gentle snore. *Good grief,* I thought. *The altitude combined with little food has gotten to him.* He had experienced some trouble when we first climbed Mount Teewinot. However, he had recovered quickly, and I had thought him well adjusted to the altitude by now. Lying awake next to what appeared to be a dead man, I was contemplating how on earth I was going to bring this dreadful news to his mother. Then Ernie had what is known all over the world as a small and sometimes embarrassing human mishap. He farted in his sleep, and I burst out laughing.

An Unusual Invitation

More hours passed without sleep. I stepped outside the tent to watch the night sky and to marvel at the stars, which seemed within arms' reach. My eyes moved along the outline of the jagged mountaintops, a black massive presence against a deep blue, almost-black sky filled with millions of blinking stars. It was breathtakingly beautiful and somehow invigorating. Standing alone on the Saddle, I felt the same tingling sensation I remembered from the beginning of my journey twelve months ago under the full moon in my canoe. All the little hairs on my body, now covered by many layers of warm clothing, reached out like antennas as if they were searching for a signal. As I stood there under the night sky, I asked to be allowed to visit the Royal Teton Retreat, to enter, so that I, too, could learn from the masters. After a little while of breathing in the beautiful night scenery around me, I crawled back into my sleeping bag to give sleep another try. And then it happened.

I found myself suddenly outside, floating in midair, looking down at our tent with Ernie and me still in it. Had I finally gone to sleep and started dreaming? I was keenly aware of my physical self lying inside my sleeping bag in the tent, yet my awareness was with the floating me. And I had company. Nearby was a presence that was also floating. I could see it, but I could not look at it directly. The being was extremely bright, and my eyes could not bear the intensity of the light. Yet I knew instantly that I trusted this being, and it was clear that I was supposed to follow it. Effortlessly we began floating toward the mountains, the same area I had scanned with my eyes not too long ago while I was marveling at the stars. We floated up the steep cliffs with ease, maybe twenty feet from the rocks, in what seemed like an instant. To hike and climb this distance and height would have taken Ernie and me many hours on foot. Floating with ease up the steep cliffs, however, made the entire rock-climbing business look pretty cumbersome and silly from my new perspective.

I enjoyed my nighttime cruise tremendously, and I was astounded at how clear my vision was in the pitch dark. I could see every detail of the rocks below and beside me. Suddenly, within the vertical cliffs, I spied a huge section shaped differently than the other rocks on the mountain. I instantly recognized it as the typical gray, meek-looking rock of spheroidal geodes. Geodes are secondary geological structures. They are generally hollow and rather plain-looking on the outside, but they hide a beautiful lining of crystals within. My favorites are raw amethyst geodes in the shape of cathedrals. I had seen and admired them as tall as three or four feet. But this area of gray geodic rock was huge. It easily spanned four hundred square feet or more. My flying companion had already passed the area and seemed to be heading to another destination. Intrigued by what I had discovered, and quick to make an irrational decision, I abandoned my companion. Ignorant of whether I would even be able to fly alone, I made a classic U-turn in midair and floated closer to my newly found interest. Sure enough, I discovered a natural break in the geodic rock the size of a small window. As I peeked through it, I drew in my breath. Through the little window, I saw a huge hall made entirely of amethyst. The floors, the walls, and the ceiling glittered in millions of shades of deep purple, illuminated by some unseen light. I could see as far as twenty to thirty yards deep into the mountain. The hall was easily about twelve feet tall. This was more beautiful than anything I had seen in my entire life. I wanted to break off a little piece of the beautiful amethyst and take it with me as a souvenir. Just as I had this disgraceful thought, I noticed that my companion had returned and was patiently waiting in midair for me to finish my inglorious plan on how to bring home some loot. I felt nothing but pure love and amusement coming from my companion. Had it been daylight, though, I am sure it would have been obvious I was blushing deeper than the deepest red of my homegrown tomatoes back in Vermont.

We continued our flight to an area of the mountain where surely no human had ever set foot. This was not because the climbing would have been particularly technical or difficult here but because poor rock quality would have made any ascent precarious and incredibly dangerous. Boulders were stacked on top of boulders, threatening to tumble at the slightest touch into the abyss of the mountain.

We were high up, thousands of feet from the ground, when I saw against the darkness of the night sky a huge area of light pouring out from between rocks and boulders in the sheer cliffs. I knew we had reached our destination, and I breathed a sigh of relief. My conscience had feared that my little detour to the amethyst cave would result in an automatic exclusion from further adventures. I was grateful that earthly rules did not seem to apply here. Later I would learn that in order to be granted entrance into one of these retreats, one had to clear one's own chakras and purify one's mind and soul on a *daily* basis. Only in this way would teachings impressed upon one's soul by the masters during retreat be able to filter through to one's subconscious and conscious mind. Through the daily practice of clearing and purification, the gap between spirit and matter could be bridged for a short time (a prerequisite for entering a retreat.) However, if the practice were not repeated daily, the gap would widen again quickly, as long as one's impurities dominated within.

It just so happened that for the last 365 days, I had been doing just that practice. I had kept track on a small scrap of paper so that I would not lose count or inadvertently skip a day. I had unfolded and folded the little paper every single day for the entire year. It had traveled with me everywhere, and it was safely tucked into a pouch of my backpack amongst my gear in our tent. I had been following a silent, inner prompting, which I credited to my untiring and ever-patient guidance. I had had no idea that my daily ritual would open doors to such incredible and exciting experiences.

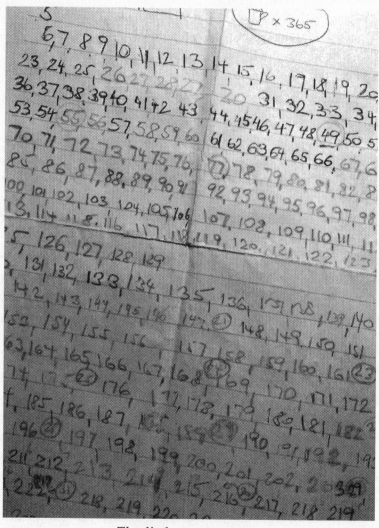

The little scrap paper
Photo: Isa Oehry

I don't remember much about the exact architecture of the retreat. But I do remember the teachings as if they had happened only a minute ago. They are deeply imprinted within my being, and I will never forget them.

I was taught that we are not what we think we are. We are not merely our physical bodies. Our bodies are tools for our higher selves to use in order to experience life in physical form. We are not the instinct either that drives our bodies and keeps them alive, regulates our physical systems, prompts our lungs to breathe, our stomachs to digest, our hearts to beat, and so much more. We are not even the intellect that allows us to analyze and reason, makes us look smart (or maybe not so smart) and allows us to express ourselves with unique personalities. The intellect, although it is hard to believe, is just another tool for us to use. So is the spiritual mind, which allows us to contemplate and understand the higher truths. The spiritual mind is also just a tool—albeit a very refined tool—that we have at our disposal while we are wandering the physical plane. We are, I was taught, in reality an expression of the Absolute. Our higher self remains entirely unaffected by our worldly experiences, whether good or bad. Forever unchanged, it exists in a permanent state of peace and harmony—a state of perfection—united and equal with all there is. We are not merely what we see. We are so much more. We are infinite and perfect beings. In our ultimate state, we simply … are.

While we experience life in physical form, we forget entirely who we really are. We don't remember that our body and mind are merely tools for expression that we can use for growth and learning on our journey back home to divine unity. We no longer have awareness that in addition to our physical body, we possess also an etheric body that houses all our memories from this lifetime and all our previous lifetimes. We forgot that we also possess a mental body that allows us to express ourselves as a unique individual, using analytical and reasoning power to create and manifest. We are not aware that we have an emotional body as well that gives us the opportunity to spread the highest vibrations of love, joy, and enthusiasm. We cannot remember that these bodies are surrounding us like nesting dolls and that they are so much larger than our tiny physical self. We have no memory that these bodies connect us like huge fields with the entire universe. All we have awareness of is our innermost, littlest nesting doll—the physical body—and we wrongly identify with it.

Identifying with our physical self leads us to believe that aches and pains inflicted upon the physical body cause our suffering and that pleasuring the senses will result in lasting well-being and happiness. Yet I was taught in the retreat that the physical body is the very last part of us to express what actually takes place on the much finer levels of our being (i.e., the much larger nesting dolls surrounding the physical body).

In order to comprehend this enormous truth and assist my overwhelmed mouse brain with fully understanding and grasping their teachings, the masters were kind enough to show me what seemed like a movie on a larger-than-life screen. On this screen I saw a rosy-cheeked infant. The baby looked healthy and seemed to be sleeping happily. I instantly fell deeply in love with it and wanted to cradle and take care of it. I was also able to see its outer bodies surrounding it like a beautiful orb consisting of fine layers of white light. It was a perfect scene of nothing but love and peace. All was obviously well in this picture. Then I saw an adult figure approaching. I could see not only his physical body but also his outer layers—his etheric, mental, and emotional bodies. These layers seemed to be on fire and looked very threatening. They were surging ahead of the man, bent into oblong shapes, reaching for the infant's peaceful orb with its delicate layers. I could see from the man's gait that he was rushing. His head was bright red. His face was filled with anger, and his features were distorted. Though I could not hear any sound, I saw his mouth moving rapidly, and I knew he was spewing forth angry and hateful words. The man's outer layers were grossly bent in an unsightly way, rushing ahead of him like a deadly wave. The moment they reached the infant's orb, the baby's eyes popped open in utter horror. Instantly its orb with its fine layers became distorted, and then the baby's entire body began to change into a disfigured being. It looked as though the life was literally being sucked out of the infant, but the man had not physically touched it.

Forgetting entirely that I was watching a scene on a screen, I rushed about in a state of desperation and panic, looking for warm water to help keep the baby alive. I instinctively understood that the baby's life was in utmost danger. Apparently water was the only thing I could come up with in that moment to protect it from the unavoidable. When I returned, still in a state of alarm, I saw that the man had left the scene and another being had come forth just in time, wrapped the little baby tenderly in a blanket, and showered it with highest vibrations of love. This love filled the entire scene, emanating an all-encompassing peace and well-being of such quality as I had never before felt or witnessed. It enveloped and uplifted me instantly. The baby's features and orb had returned to their peaceful and perfect state. It was again rosy-cheeked, sleeping happily. I breathed a huge sigh of relief.

When I finally relaxed after my emotional roller-coaster ride, I began to realize and understand what I had seen on the screen. I had been shown this out-of-control behavior in order to witness and observe the outer, much finer layers and the powerful effects they have. The negativity spewed forth by the adult figure caused his uncontrolled bodies to run wild, distort, agitate, and build up intense pressure. These pressure-filled bodies were surging far ahead of him, seeking a target for release. The moment his outer layers reached the orb of the unprotected and peacefully sleeping child, the baby's fine outer layers reacted, and its physical body responded with shock and almost instantaneous distortion. It was clear that had it not been rescued, it would have perished.

I understood that it is what originates within these much finer layers of ourselves in the form of thoughts and emotions that affects us deeply and ultimately transforms our physical body. The physical body is the very last (the smallest of all the nesting dolls) to respond to the state of the outer layers. That the anger was purposefully directed toward the baby or that the uncontrolled anger found the baby to be an easy target for release was irrelevant. It was clear to me that negativity and anger are emotions powerful enough to kill an unguarded soul. Once unleashed, they search for a target regardless of the target's ability or inability to fend off such an assault.

I witnessed the outer layers of the baby change and respond, its body mirroring the destructive effects *without the man ever physically touching it*. I saw the layers in various stages, and even as an observer, I deeply experienced their effects. First I witnessed them in a state of peace and harmony, which filled me instantly with deep happiness. Then I witnessed the effects of those layers dangerously charged, and that experience immediately threw me into a state of panic. Because the layers were made visible to me, I could actually see with my own eyes that we are so much more than our physical body. And by being able to observe the layers' various shapes, colors, and behaviors, I was able to see what is usually invisible to the eyes—how our thoughts and emotions express themselves.

Before I knew what was happening, my exciting nocturnal outing was over. I found myself back in the tent next to Ernie. His sleeping bag was moving rhythmically with his breathing—no dead man this time. I had plenty to think about for the rest of the night. Sleep was the last thing I worried about now.

THE MESSAGE

I woke Ernie, who had enjoyed a good night's sleep, at the first sign of dawn. It was a cold morning with an icy northwesterly breeze. Our hats were pulled low down to our eyes. The east face of the Grand, beautifully lit by the first rays of morning sun, glistened and sparkled with a thin layer of glaze ice—verglas. Though we knew the verglas would probably melt in the course of the morning hours, it was clear it would be a bitter-cold and windy climb should we try the Exum Ridge again. With this in mind, we decided to go with our backup plan and give the Middle Teton a try. The Saddle connects to the Middle Teton at its northwest ice couloir. This route was also exposed to the bitter-cold northerly winds and most likely covered in ice. To stay out of the wind and hopefully enjoy some sunshine, we opted for the southwest couloir on the other side of the massive Middle Teton.

Ernie preparing an early morning breakfast with
Middle Teton glacier in background
Photo: Isa Oehry

We shared the last spoonfuls of oats, broke camp, and descended to the Meadows, located at 9,300 feet. From there we began the long ascent to the Saddle of the Middle Teton. It was an arduous approach, as we had to first hike up the cumbersome scree past the glacier moraines and then around the base of the massive mountain to reach the beginning of the southwest couloir.

When we finally arrived at the Saddle of the Middle Teton, we could see the peak, it seemed to be as far away as the moon. We were out of food, and the going was slow. The mountain demanded that we earn each step and foot of elevation. As we progressed steadily upward, my mind was fully occupied with the details of my previous night's adventure. To my astonishment, I was still going despite the lack of sleep and food. By now I must have been past my second wind—and possibly my third or fourth, if such things even exist. I heard Ernie mutter something incomprehensible below me. When I asked him if everything was all right, he indicated that he could not speak. Worried that the altitude might have toyed with him again, I waited until he caught up with me. "Hungry" was the only word he could mutter. Feeling guilty and responsible for our inadequate food supply, I took my pack down and rummaged around in the hope that there was something edible in it. To my surprise, I was successful. Well, sort of. With a big smile, I produced a little tube that contained some interesting-looking goop. It was a tiny sample of maybe two teaspoons, a free handout I had been given some time ago. Apparently endurance athletes scarf this stuff. We shared it equally. One tiny suck for each of us, and it was gone. But for Ernie it seemed to do the trick. He suddenly forged ahead with newly found energy and disappeared from sight. Slowly but steadily I worked my way up the crown of the mountain and finally reached its breathtaking peak, where Ernie awaited me with a huge smile and a big hug.

Just to sit on such an exposed peak, thousands of feet above any level ground, is worth all the effort and pain. The peak of the Middle Teton is nothing less than spectacular. We were excited and happy as we enjoyed our exposed perch in plenty of sunshine and without any wind. Looking down on the Exum Ridge of the Grand, we were glad we had changed our plans this morning. The ridge was still engulfed in a thick layer of cloud and only visible when the stiff and cold northwesterly wind, which continued to force its way through the Lower Saddle of the Grand, blew open a little window.

The growling of our stomachs demanded our attention, and we decided to begin the long descent of thousands of feet of altitude and several long miles back to our car. This time gravity was on our side. All we needed to do was move one foot forward, and gravity did the rest. We retreated, however, almost as slowly as we had climbed, making sure no rocks were set loose to trundle into the couloir below. Once we reached the Saddle of the Middle Teton, we were able to move freely.

Ernie had conjured up a plan while down-climbing the couloir. The moment he reached the parking lot several miles down in the valley, where he had left his cell phone, he would make a call to Dornans, the only restaurant in the vicinity. He would order practically the entire menu for us, including some extra cheesecake to top it off, for immediate pickup. With this prospect in mind, he apparently found new strength, descending at an impressive trot way ahead of me.

I continued to move slowly but steadily, making my way down the glacier moraines to the Meadows. Exhaustion finally overcame me. I was tired and hungry, and my mind was filled to the brim with all I had experienced. As I slowly walked down the narrow trail, I recalled the beginning of this journey under the blue moon. I remembered the prompting I had felt, inviting me to an unknown destination, to a mysterious world concealing ancient wisdom. I thought of how I knew instantly that searching for the origin of this prompting would be a worthwhile endeavor, but I had no idea what hidden truths would be revealed to me. During this past year, I was granted glimpses of the many qualities of prana. I had begun to understand its immense potential to transform us so that we could reach a state of perfect health and vitality. I had learned of its ability to bring clarity to our minds so that we could understand truths previously beyond our comprehension. And, in so many different ways I was taught how I could accomplish this feat. The search for this nourishment led me to understand my personal path and the reasons for my existence. I understood my struggles and their origin. I also had been granted glimpses at our potential as human beings. I knew now that with all possibilities already in existence, we have, once control of thoughts and emotions is learned, the opportunity to rapidly evolve so that we can create and manifest beyond our wildest dreams. I recognized our world as a truly remarkable place, offering infinite opportunities. I wished not to let one single day in my life come and go without being aware of my higher self and its potential.

I continued my slow but steady pace, mind and body tired, eyes fixed on the rocky path so I would not stumble and fall. My empty tummy protested, reminding me with anticipation about the smorgasbord Ernie was organizing for us. I had left the glacier moraines behind, and I was carefully making my way down the sharp and cumbersome scree. Without glacial ice, my surroundings were again nothing but gray rock. I was alone on the path. Suddenly I was overcome with a deep sense of gratitude for the guidance I had been granted over the past year and all that I had been taught during my waking as well as sleeping hours. It was a feeling so strong that I thought my chest would burst open and my heart would jump out and run away in search of someone, anyone to hug.

I stopped for a moment and took a deep breath. As I stood, I lifted my eyes off the trail, and there, a few feet before me on a bolder the size of a garage, I saw the answer to my plea. It was a beautiful heart of silver mica about ten inches tall, sparkling in the sun. It shimmered like starlight, as if powered by some unseen force. I was so taken aback by its sudden appearance that I faltered and swayed, nearly falling and landing myself in the sharp scree. I will forever remember the exact location of this beautiful message.

The message
Photo: Isa Oehry

EPILOGUE

I knew that what I had learned and witnessed during my one-year journey (and visit to the Royal Teton Retreat) was true. However, I still longed to "see it with my own eyes" while firmly grounded in our three-dimensional reality. While I was editing the many notes from my journey, I came across a study conducted by Dr. Emoto. He had used rice to prove the effect thoughts and emotions have on our physical reality (i.e., how our intentions can actually impact and change molecular structures). I set out to duplicate Emoto's experiment.

In March of 2014, I boiled three cups of white rice. I also sterilized two canning jars of equal size together with their lids in a pot of boiling water. Carefully I divided the rice into equal portions and filled the two jars. I then sealed them and waited for the rice to cool off. The following day I took the jars and marked one with the words "You fool" and the other with the words "I love you." I also wrote the date on each lid. I then opened both jars to break the seal and let oxygen and bacteria infiltrate. I closed the lids slightly, enough to keep them from falling off but not enough to seal the jars. The goal was for air to move in and out of the jars. I placed them in the same room where they were exposed to the same amount of light. They sat about four feet apart from each other. From then on, I began for roughly one or two minutes each day to send feelings of love to the jar with the words "I love you" written on it. I simply ignored the jar marked with the words "You fool." Over the following weeks and months, I took the lids off both jars every two weeks or so to have a peek. I made a point in opening both jars always for the same amount of time. At times I would travel away from my home for a couple of days and leave the jars behind. At one time I abandoned the jars for three weeks while I went on a trip to Europe.

The jar with the words "You fool" responded predictably. Its contents began a gradual process of decomposition as you would expect if you left food out in the open. The rice turned a nasty brown color, forming little mushroom shapes of mold.

The rice in the jar with the words "I love you" (to my utter astonishment) remained white. As I am writing these words, eleven months since the beginning of the experiment, the rice in the jar marked with the words "I love you" is still as white as snow.

| The jar with the words "You fool" | The jar with the words "I love you" |

Photos: Isa Oehry

Scientifically this is impossible. It is, however, concrete evidence of the power of love displaying itself in front of my eyes. Our emotions are indeed powerful beyond our imagination.

Scholastic Research Topics

Prana—Light Energy

Global Advocacy Group—One Laptop per Child (OLPC)

Morphic Field—Rupert Sheldrake

Rat Learning Experiment—William McDougall

Plant Consciousness/Plant Communication—Cleve Backster, Ted Farmer, Richard Karban

Double Slit Experiment/The Observer Effect —Quantum Physics

Cell Memory—Bruce Lipton

The Human Genome Project

Brain Research—John Lorber

Visualization/Law of Attraction—Rhonda Byrne

Hypnotherapy—Albert Mason

Schumann Resonance—Winfried Schumann

Global Coherence Initiative—Institute of HeartMath

Sunspots—A. L. Tchijevsky

Creation of Memory—David Hamilton

Attachment/Nonattachment—Buddhism

Language of Water—Masaru Emoto

Power of Sexuality—Elisabeth Haich

BIBLIOGRAPHY

Aïvanhov, Omraam M. *Das Buch der Göttlichen Magie.* Germany: Prosveta Verlag, 1997.

Andrews, T. *How to See and Read the Aura.* Woodbury: Llewellyn Publications, 2010.

Ascended Master Teaching Foundation. *Daily Meditations.* Mount Shasta, CA: Saint Germain Press, 1995.

Backster, C. *Primary Perception: Biocommunication with Plants, Living Foods, and Human Cells.* Anza, CA: White Rose Millennium Press, 2003.

Ballard, Guy W. *Unveiled Mysteries: Secrets of the Comte de Saint Germain.* http://www.forgottenbooks.org: Forgotten Books, 2008.

Braden, G. *Fractal Time.* Carlsbad, CA: Hay House, Inc., 2009.

Braden, G. *The Isaiah Effect.* New York: Random House, Inc., 2000.

Byrne, R. *The Secret.* Hillsboro, OR: Beyond Words Publishing, 2006.

Emoto, M. *The Hidden Messages in Water.* Hillsboro, OR: Beyond Words Publishing, Inc., 2004.

Flint, G.A. *Healing Your Mind and Soul: Therapeutic Interventions in Quantum Reality.* La Vergne, TN: Lightning Source. Inc., 2012.

Global Coherence Initiative. "Earth Rhythms," last modified March 25, 2015, http://www.heartmath.org.

Grasser, H. (producer), and P. A. Staubinger (director). *Am Anfang War Das Licht.* Vienna, Austria: Allegro Film, 2011.

Haich, E. *Initiation.* Santa Fe, NM: Aurora Press, Inc., 2000.

Haich, E. *Sexuelle Kraft und Yoga.* Ergolding, Deutschland: Drei Eichen Verlag, 1990.

Hamilton, David R. *It's the Thought that Counts: Why Mind over Matter Really Works.* Carlsbad, CA: Hay House, Inc., 2005.

Hilarion. (1986). *The Golden Quest.* Ontario, Canada, Marcus Books.

Larson, Christian D. *Leave It to God.* Camarillo, CA: DeVorss & Company, 1940.

Lipton, B. *The Biology of Belief.* Carlsbad, CA: Hay House, Inc., 2005.

Lipton, B., and S. Bhaerman. *Spontaneous Evolution.* Carlsbad, CA: Hay House, Inc., 2010.

Lloyd, A., and B. Johnson. *Healing Code.* New York: Grand Central Life & Style, Hachette Book Group, 2010.

Meister Saint Germain. *Goldene Regeln.* Berlin, Germany: Die Brücke zur Freiheit e.V., 1995.

Motz, J. "Everyone an Energy Healer: The TREAT V Conference in Santa Fe." *Advances: Journal of the Institute for the Advancement of Health* Vol. 9 (1993): pp. 95-98.

Oschman, Jim, and Nora Oschman. "Science Measures the Human Energy Field," last modified 2015, http://www.reiki.org.

Pearsall, Paul. *The Heart's Code: Tapping the Wisdom and Power of Our Heart Energy.* New York, NY: Random House, Inc., 1998.

Peer, Wendy. "Protein Study Shows Evolutionary Link between Plants, Humans," last modified February 15, 2010, http://www.purdue.edu.

Playfair, Guy Lyon. *If This Be Magic: The Forgotten Power of Hypnosis.* Hove, UK: White Crow Books, 2011.

Prophet, E. C. *Stain Germain: Master Alchemist.* Gardiner, MT, Summit University Press, 2004.

Prophet, M. L., and E. C. Prophet. *Saint Germain on Alchemy – Formulas for Self-Transformation.* Corwin Springs, MT: Summit University Press, 1984, 1993.

Prophet, M. L., and E. C. Prophet. *The Masters and their Retreats.* Corwin Springs, MT: Summit University Press, 2003.

Ramacharaka, Yogi *Raja Yoga or Mental Development.* Chicago: The Yogi Publication Society, 1934.

Remen, R. N. *Aus Liebe zum Leben*. New York: Riverhead Books, 2000.

Smith, V. *Living with Your Light Turned On*. Rumney, NH: Vales End, 2013.

Spalding, B. T. *Life and Teaching of the Master of the Far East*. Camarillo, CA: DeVorss & Company, 1996.

Stein-Luthke, L., and M. F. Luthke. *Balancing the Light Within*. Chagrin Falls, OH: Expansion Publishing, 1995.

Szepes, Maria. *The Red Lion: The Elixir of Eternal Life*. Yelm, WA: Horus Publishing, Inc., 1997.

Talbot, David. "Given Tablets but No Teachers, Ethiopian Children Teach Themselves," last modified October 29, 2012, http://www.technologyreview.com.

Talbot, Michael. *Beyond the Quantum*. London: Macmillian Publishing Company, 1986.

Tompkins, Peter, and Christopher Bird. *Das Geheime Leben der Pflanzen*. Frankfurt am Main, Deutschland: Fischer Taschenbuch GmbH, 1997.

Vivekananda, S. *Rāja-Yoga*. New York: Ramakrishna-Vivekananda Center, 1973.

Walker, E. H. *The Physics of Consciousness*. New York: Perseus Publishing, 2000.

Werner, M., and Stöckli, T. *Life from Light*. Forest Row, England: Clairview Books, 2007.

Williams, David. "The Blue Moon," last modified December 11, 2003, http://www.nssdc.gsfc.nasa.gov.

Yesudian, S., and Haich, E. *Yoga, Uniting East and West.* New York: Harper & Brothers, 1956.

Ziegler, Bodhigyan G. *Tarot Spiegel der Seele.* Neuhausen, Deutschland: Urania Verlags AG, 1988.

Zyga, Lisa. "World's Largest Quantum Bell Test Spans Three Swiss Towns," last modified June 16, 2008, http://www.phys.org.

About the Author

Isabella S. Oehry, was born and raised in the small European country sandwiched between Austria and Switzerland, the Principality of Liechtenstein. After an education in business, Oehry traveled extensively and eventually settled in Vermont, which is sometimes called the Liechtenstein of the United States. She continued her education and earned a degree in management information systems. But her strong interests in the mystery of the human mind and man's untapped potential prompted her to pursue an advanced degree in psychology with a specialization in clinical mental health.

For more information you can visit her website at <u>www.isaoehry.com</u>.

Chickadee

Inquisitive, happy, free,
Bright of eye, always smiling,
Taking flight amongst many spirits
Tree to ground,
Blue skies, gray,
Snow and wind, driving rain,
Still bright of eye,
Unafraid
Curious.
Content? I think not.
A world she sees, not eyed by most.
Wings spread—
to air, to sky, to—

—XO BB

This poem was dedicated to Isa Oehry
and printed by permission of its author,
who wishes to remain anonymous.

From the daily prana distribution ritual during Isa Oehry's one year journey, documented in *Under A Blue Moon,* the following powerful meditation was born:

Prana Meditation – Healing through Light Energy

Photo: Isa Oehry

Printed in the United States
By Bookmasters